THE PRIMITIVE CULTURE OF INDIA

BY

COLONEL T.C. HODSON

GYAN

Published by

Gyan Publishing House
5, Ansari Road
Daryaganj, New Delhi-110002
Phone: 011-47034999, 9811692060
E-mail: books@gyanbooks.com

Distribution Network
gyanbooks.com
India, USA, Canada, UK, Australia

ISBN: 978-93-6433-649-9 (HB)
First Published, 1922

2nd Impression 2024

Printed at: Gyan Press, Delhi.

THE PRIMITIVE CULTURE OF INDIA
AUTHOR: COLONEL T.C. HODSON

THE PRIMITIVE CULTURE OF INDIA

THE PRIMITIVE CULTURE OF INDIA

THE PRIMITIVE CULTURE OF INDIA

Lectures delivered in 1922 at

The School of Oriental Studies (Univ. of London)

BY

COLONEL T. C. HODSON

(Late Indian Civil Service)

1922

LECTURE I.

COMPLEXITY OF INDIAN CULTURE.

Complexity of Indian Culture—Analysis of Fundamental Elements—Dream Values and Social Life—Prepotency of the Past—Mind and Body—Belief in Reincarnation—Language as a Social Product—Assimilation of Customs and the Relations of Higher with Lower Culture—Value *in situ* of Customs—The Selective and Comparative Method—Common Elements and Range of Variable Elements.

Before I attempt to define the lower culture or to describe its geographical distribution in India, let me clear the ground by emphasising the fact that primitive characters are not to be looked for in Indian culture as it now is for " existing savage races are not merely peoples who have been left behind in the stream of progress. They are not simply examples of early stages in the development of human culture beyond which other peoples have progressed. It can be shown that each one of them has a highly complex history in which rites and customs introduced from elsewhere, perhaps from some highly-advanced society, have blended with others of a really primitive or infantile kind. . . . Though existing cultures may not be primitive in the sense that they represent simple and uncontaminated stages of social development, we can safely accept the primitive character of their mentality and take them as guides to the history of mental development, though they are of very questionable value as guides to the order of social development." **(1a)**. We must therefore dismiss from our minds such catch words as arrested development or continuity of progress. Let us remember the antiquity of India, the complexity of its social groupings, and the immense range of its culture.

ELEMENTS.

We are all psychologists nowadays. True, the psyche is seldom mentioned in the discussions of this rigorous science. As I look for the elements of the mental make-up of folk in the lower culture, I find their attitude characterised by the dominance of tradition, and I can ask you from my own knowledge to accept the view put forward by Dr. Rivers whose eminence as a psychologist is as secure as his distinction both as an anthropologist and a historian of the past of human societies. From his personal knowledge of the lower culture in India, in Melanesia and the Torres Straits, he finds that " it is a striking feature of ethnographical investigation among people of lowly culture that it is impossible to obtain any rational explanation of rites and customs even when such explanation would seem to us obvious. The people are content to follow without question their social customs and to practise the often highly elaborate rites of their religion merely because it has been so ordained by their fathers " (2). For my part I think the lack of rational explanations of institutions or customs can be associated with the value assigned to dream experiences. Thus " The Tangkhuls say that a man who is attacked by a buffalo will lose any lawsuit in which he happens at that time to be involved. They also believe that if a man dreams that he is attacked by a buffalo, he will suffer similar misfortune. They attach to the dream precisely the same significance as to the actual event. Does this mean that their dreams are as substantial and possess the same measure of reality as the facts of their waking vision ? If this conclusion were legitimate on these facts, the dream life would have a continuity with the waking life and possess a specific reality for them. The interpretation of unusual dreams is left to the maiba or to some wise old man."(3)

With the Andamanese there are " certain individuals known as oko-pai. ad (lit a dreamer) who are credited with the possession of supernatural powers such as second sight and of a mysterious influence over the fortunes and lives of their neighbours." He exploits his reputation thoroughly and must show proof from time to time of his power. He can bespeak property which then is not available for presentation to anyone else. He is " credited with the power of communicating in dreams with the invisible powers of good and evil and also of seeing the spirits of the departed or of those who are ill." **(3a)**

Among the Sema Nagas **(3b)** " there are probably many other forms of genna practised by the *thumomi* who, indeed, probably invent new forms of whatever kind and whenever they see fit." He is an interpreter of omens, a dreamer, clairvoyant. . . . Dreams, like omens, are not the exclusive province of the *thumomi*, and happen to anyone. Indeed, most Semas believe in their own dreams and take note of them as forecasting events to come, in particular those of hunting and war." Throughout this area we find a constant belief in and attribution of authority and prestige to those who dream dreams, who see visions, and are thereby known to be in touch with sources of power external to the individual.

Of the Kols, it is said that " Daher gibt der Kol viel auf Träume weil seine Seele im Schlafe heller sieht and mit der Geisterwelt verkehrt, die ihr im wachen Zustande mehr oder minder verschlossen ist. . . . Träume sind dem Kol Offenbarungen aus der Geisterwelt " **(4)**. I take these cases as samples of the ample evidence that " many peoples still trust greatly to the value of dreams as guides to the ordering of their daily conduct "**(5)**. The dream " the form in which experience becomes manifest in sleep " has " the characters of infancy " which modern psychology regards as " due to the removal in sleep of the higher controlling levels " **(6)**. The determination of conduct by reference to experience divested of higher controls, especially when that class of experience is deemed of special value, will help to understand the behaviour—using that word in a large sense—of the lower culture. Yet we must confess that " the determination of social behaviour by the unconscious is not confined to rude culture but is only somewhat more obvious in it than among more highly civilised peoples " (7). Further, in the practice of referring unusual dream experiences to " some wise old man," we see a means whereby the wise old man may influence traditional evaluations to his own advantage or to the advantage of his own class, and a means by which the continuity of tradition can be secured from excessive inroads of novel ideas. That changes in and modifications of important elements of the social fabric have occurred from time to time is certain even in the most lowly groups, and we thus can realise how these changes can be effected.

These beliefs have a real objective existence. They are therefore proper material for examination. They are associated with and form part of a whole of an organically inter-related interdependent corpus or mass of traditional institutions and customs, which cover the whole field of social activity. How vast that field is we may realise by remembering that " an elaborate philosophy " (8) has been evolved by the least advanced Australian group. Systems in their way no less elaborate are to be found among groups of the lower culture in India. The traditional views, as we regard them, are in truth living forces, harmonised, or tending to be harmonised, by social continuity with all other manifestations of social activity, because these beliefs are lived rather than thought out, *veçus plûtôt que pensées*. What we regard as traditional and unreasoned, because it appears unreasonable to us, is in the lower culture viewed as reasonable and valid, even more authoritative and important than the data which with us serve as the basis of reasoning. Thus in framing our definition of the lower culture—from a psychological aspect—we must assign due weight to these factors—the dominance of tradition or custom and the superior validity allowed to experiences—dreams, hyperaesthetic apparitions and the like—which seem to spring from the liberation of the unconscious elements of mind from the controls imposed by education and normal life. The formation of special interests and values by these processes deserves attention as a possible source of other cultural features. The actions and reactions of the lower culture with its physical environment are affected by these habits. " Environment " is more than the physical environment (**9**), complex and difficult of analysis as that is. The society in which we live and move and have our being is part of our environment. The past—agelong as it is—forms part of our environment, for it is active in shaping the conditions as well as our institutions of the present. The prepotency of the past is a characteristic of the lower culture. Current in the lower culture are ideas as to the nature of man, psychological ideas they may be called, which express clearly after the manner of the lower culture an unmistakable recognition as well as an explanation of the dominion of the past. The ideas we form of the nature of the physical environment, of the nature of our relations with the physical environment, with our fellow-beings, both with those who constitute our society and those who are members of other societies in contact with our own, affect and help to determine our behaviour. We know that the processes of forgetting—of unwitting repression—are not less important, not less worthy of critical investigation than those of memory (**10**). The student of human culture finds matter for study in the processes which produce stagnation, even retrogression, which cause the abandonment of useful arts (**11**), which cause societies to refuse to adopt new modes of life—calculated and proved to be —of greater efficiency—judged by material results—than the old and traditional methods (**11a**), which have the support of sanctions ordinarily classified as religious —in reality—tradition, nothing else.

These are " witting repressions " which—assuming the well-known form of the *tabu*, impose restrictions on human activity sometimes of an absurd nature often of serious economic disadvantage, as when people place a ban on milk, a most valuable form of aliment (**11b**). All these are the fruits of the reactions, under the dominance of tradition, of man's mental activity with his environment. Let us remember—what in a purely mechanistic explanation of psychology we might overlook—that, after all, " Institutions are the effects not the causes of mental traits,"(**12**), and " It was the machinery of the brain which discovered the uses of fire and iron; found out the elements which compose the earth, sun and stars; discovered the laws which regulate the movements of planets. . . . Nothing is too small and nothing too great to fall within the compass of its machinery " (**13**).

It is mind that matters most. I remember that I was shown the war stone at Maikel, and was told the tale of the woman who inadvertently and by an accident saw the sacred thing. She died as the result of her imprudence. Col. Shakespear tells how "A Lushai named Kela visited Aijal; on the road he met a rat which stood up in the middle of the road and held its paws to its head. 'What a curious rat,' he said. Two days after he reached his home he died. To see such a rat is certainly '*thianglo*.' This incident happened a short time ago; no one had ever heard of such a rat having been seen before and the unusualness of the occurrence coupled with the death of Kela was, to the Lushais, proof positive of its being the cause of his death " (**13a**). There are wereleopards and weretigers among the Semas, men and women whose soul passes into a tiger or leopard; during sleep the soul is the leopard with its full faculties, but the man dies as soon as he hears " that his leopard body has been killed. The son of Yemithi of Lizotomi whose leopard body was killed at Sagami, heard the news as he was returning to his village, and expired on the spot for no other reason. A curious example of the power of the Sema mind over the Sema body." **(13b)**

REINCARNATION BELIEFS.

It is not enough to assert dogmatically that the lower culture is what it is because it is dominated by tradition. Proof is required, and that proof must show the existence of some social idea or belief which, as the core of all social beliefs and the institutions which represent these beliefs in action, can be regarded as capable of explaining how tradition has assumed the dominance assigned to it. That social idea or belief I find to be the belief in reincarnation, the belief that society is composed of constantly recurring units so that the activities of these units, their relations one with another, their social duties and liabilities, are always regulated by reference to the tradition of the activities, the relations, the duties and liabilities of those deceased members of the social group who are regarded as having returned to the group in their persons. "I am my grandfather," says this belief. "Therefore I act and behave in all social contingencies as my grandfather behaved. If in any contingency I am confronted by a novelty, by a combination of circumstances which it would seem had not presented itself to my grandfather, I consult those old men of the group whose knowledge of my grandfather exceeds mine and by their interpretation of the circumstances I am guided to the action which is appropriate to the personality of my grandfather." Such is the line of thought. I shall show how the system of social education in the lower culture is, and can only be, inspired by traditionalism, how the idea of reincarnation, the constant succession of identical units, affects all expressions, simple and complex, of social activity, inspires and explains social structure and is the cardinal ideal of social life. Where ancestor-worship makes its appearance, whether as in some measure in descent from the idea of reincarnation or as the result of other factors, it is obviously an element of prepotency in the determination of social values in the direction of tradition. Thus there are ideas still active in shaping the institutions of the lower culture which derive their strength from, as they lend their support to, social forces of the traditional order and structure.

The great vehicle of tradition is society. Tradition is society and society is tradition. The human units which compose society change constantly, even rapidly. The changes which society undergoes are slower—less perceptible—and therefore society appears to be immobile—changeless—but there are limits to social memory, there are variations. The dominance of tradition is the dominance of society over the individual **(13a)**. Therefore it is in group life that its dominance in the lower culture can be best studied. This dominance is, after all, a question of degree, for we are all to some extent under the social law **(14)**. The unit of our study is the group. The strength of group life can be well shown by Indian examples.

GROUP SOLIDARITY.

We learn from a Settlement Officer, who some years ago investigated the condition of the wretched people who had not been included in the great Reserve where exploitation by the landlord is impossible, that "the Sonthal does not regard himself as a separate unit but as part and parcel of the village community whose head and representative with the outisde world is the Manjhi **(15)**. As he says in a further passage, "It has been remarked by officers experienced in the ways of the Sonthals that the village community is socially the unit amongst the Sonthals, not the individual" **(16)**. Of the Nagas in Manipur, years ago I found that "What gives validity to these unwritten laws is the vague fear that something may happen if they are broken. Something, this terrible death of a tribesman has happened. Why did it happen? What more logical than the answer that it happened because a sin has been committed. . . . There is always the disturbing thought that not always nor of necessity does the sinner bear the punishment of his sin and the genna system is strengthened, social solidarity is maintained, by the idea of vicarious punishment which makes it the business of each man to see that his neighbour keeps the law" **(17)**.

Among the Nagas of the north are found similar social tabus. One is reminded, says Mr. Hutton **(17a)** of the reason given by some Semas for reaping by hand only, because one man once slashed his stomach and killed himself when reaping with a dao. . . . How easily such a notion may spring up can be gathered from a single instance which came under my notice of a tabu on an Angami. I was going up from Zubza to Kohima with Srisalhu, of Khonoma, when we met a large snake in the road. I started to beat it, but Srisalhu would not join in. When I had killed it, he said that it was kenna for him to kill snakes. The reason was that his home in Khonoma, or rather his father's home, had been inhabited by a snake. When Srisalhu removed to a new site, the snake appeared in the new house. (It might easily be transferred from one building to another in a dhule or paddy or in part of the thatch). It still lives in Srisalhu's house and is frequently seen, having survived two rebuildings. This fact impressed Srisalhu, who talked it over with the other men of his kindred, who considered that a man who had a snake like that in his house ought not to kill snakes at all. Accordingly it is now regarded as kenna for Srisalhu and his household to kill snakes. If Srisalhu's descendants are prolific, this kenna will doubtless in time affect a whole kindred."

LANGUAGES.

To turn to another manifestation of social activity, to the means of communication, I may remind you that twenty years ago a great scientific task was carried out by Sir George Grierson, viz., the Linguistic Survey of India. To complete the analysis of the essential characteristics of the lower culture I must assay the material yielded by those splendid investigations. Let us not forget that "Le langage a pour premiere condition l'existence des societès humaines dont il est de son côte l'instrument indispensable et constamment employè ; . . . le langage est donc éminemment un fait social. En effet il entre exactement dans la definition qu'a proposée M. Durkheim ; une langue existe independamment de chacun des individus qui la parlent, et bien qu'elle n'ait aucune réalitè en dehors de la somme des individus en question, elle est cependant, outre sa generalitè, extérieure à chacun d'eux : ce qui le montre, c'est qu'il ne depend d'aucun d'eux de la changer et que toute déviation de l'usage provoque une réaction **(18)**. Language-sounds, produced and varied and controlled by the will acting on the organs of speech, lips, oral cavity, teeth, tongue, nasal cavity, uvula and throat, organs whose primary use is the ingestion and mastication and preparation of food, involve a convention between speaker and hearer as to the significance of the sounds so formed. Il faut parler le même langage. We may study languages under the aspect of their phonetics, the sounds peculiar to each social group, of their structure, for there is no one sealed pattern. We may analyse their vocabularies, the words or sounds which by social convention are attached to specific ideas and things. We cannot overlook their general characters, their power of meeting new ideas with new words or new combinations of familiar words, their power of getting behind the multiplicity of sensation and achieving—however partially—a classification which is abstraction of general qualities. We know that experts are now busy on the scientific record of the phonetics of the Indian languages, we know that unusual combinations of sounds are to be found in common use in many social groups in India, perhaps vestigial evidence of minute physical differences of the structure of the vocal organs. We learn that there is a great diversity of structure in Indian languages, ranging from a wonderful complexity to monosyllabic simplicity; that there are many devices, tones, generic determinatives, couplets and combinations, infixes, prefixes, suffixes, which Indian social groups employ to eke out the material—scanty enough in many cases—which tradition has allowed them. They would utter the thoughts that arise and there are no words. There are vocabularies which, like those of the primitive languages of the New World **(19)**, are marked by a number of independent words each expressing some variation, often minute, of some action, or each expressing a different object which we should describe by a class name **(20)**.

They are marked again like the languages of the New World by a strong personalisation which clings to the parts of the body and the members of the social group **(21)**. as shown by the use of pronominal affixes. Whether or not in this phenomenon we may see the influence of the development of individual as opposed to communal possession is a matter for thought and consideration **(22)**. What is certain is that language—preserved by methods of tradition—retains the impress of social conditions even when those conditions have ceased and that language is determined by social conditions, reflects them and describes them.

MATERIAL CULTURE.

In the domain of material culture, which I define as the expression of the social activities in utilising or—what is more significant—refusing to utilise the properties of the products of their immediate physical environment;

I seek the distinctive characteristic of the lower culture in the attitudes taken up in regard to the natural resources on which they are dependent for their means of livelihood. There are still groups where agriculture is not practised, where the weapons of the chase are the products of nature, stones, sticks, bows whose strings are sinews, where the dominion of nature is almost absolute. But there are many degrees in the lower culture. If a group in its material activities refuses experiment, declines the trial of new methods, and is illiberal of naturalisation towards fresh attitudes, it is in jeopardy of stagnation, even of retrogression, it must be assigned to the lower culture. Thus we return to the general position that the essential characteristic of the lower culture is the habit of mind which, dominated exclusively by tradition, refers all novel experiences to traditional forms, which adapts introduced rites or customs only by so modifying them that they lose their vigour of novelty and " acquire the primitive or infantile character of the culture which assimilates them " **(23)**. We may at times witness this process of denaturalisation and assimilation, for there some cases where the new idea can be assimilated only by a modification of the structure of the culture into which it has been introduced. These moments of partial assimilation—of social indigestion—are often disruptive to a far greater extent than we might expect. They mark a stage in progress. Since all cultures, lower as well as higher, have an immense history behind them, we may expect to find in them both survivals, that is to say, organs which still retain their individuality and functions and have therefore achieved some measure of congruity and harmony with the general social organisation, as well as vestigial customs, which we may regard as once active, even essential, but not obsolete and meaningless, which survive **(24)** solely because they satisfy some aesthetic need or because they are harmless and purely neutral in social value.

Whether we can ever ascertain the general principles on which assimilation proceeds is hardly probable. Each case has to be considered on its merits. It may be we shall find that in India, as in Australia (**24a**) " if two races are at a decidedly different level of culture . . . , it is extremely improbable that there would be any amalgamation on equal terms. The weaker and less cultured would certainly be exterminated by the stronger and more highly cultured." Contact does not always or of necessity involve amalgamation. Imitation, with the limitations of differences of speech and of material resources, there has been in plenty, since the prestige of the superior culture leads surely to this. In the process of imitation we may expect to find that much that was vital in the original models has been lost, transformed and metamorphosed so that the compromise formations which result do not resemble either originals in essentials, in analogy to the results in the human world of marriages across a racial frontier (**24b**).

That there has been, that there is still, peaceful penetration of the lower by the higher culture, is undeniable. But it is also true that there have been violent destructions of social groups of the lower by the higher, of the higher by the lower. Indian history is full of such cases. The conditions requisite for " amalgamation of two cultures on equal terms " cannot be laid down definitely, but there are many facts with which we are not now specifically concerned, to indicate that the effects of the interpenetration of cultures which, by reason of its long history, characterises Indian culture as a whole, are not less manifest in modifications of the social attitudes of the higher culture than in those of the lower culture.

METHOD.

" To see life steadily and to see it whole " is no bad maxim for the student of the lower culture, for each custom must be interpreted as part of a whole, in the light of the nature of the whole of which it is a part (**25**). Each custom derives support and validity from all the other customs of the whole, and gives support and validity in its turn to them. Sir Laurence Gomme warned us long years ago that " We must know the exact position of each item before we begin to compare, or we may be comparing absolutely unlike things. Customs and rites which are alike in practice can be shown to have originated from quite different causes, to express quite different motifs and cannot, therefore, be held to belong to a common class" (**26**). This warning is specially applicable to Indian conditions. Convergence is undeniable in some cases, such as female infanticide. It is easy to select a fact recorded by a perfectly competent and impartial observer and by neglecting the context to find what is wanted. Qui sait trouver sait chercher. The comparative method in unscientific hands becomes the selective method and is open to the criticism which Sir Laurence Gomme passed on it. The only way is to treat the social life as a psychological unity just as, in the study of the psychology of individuals, the whole man is taken as the unit for investigation. That means we have to ascertain the degree of congruity which any custom belief or institution has with the general mental life of the group and with the whole body of rites, customs and institutions to determine whether it is in organic harmony with them or is a survival, retaining some validity and utility, not altogether out of harmony with the general activities, or is to be classed as vestigial, existing solely because it does no harm, and tolerated so long, and only so long, as it is harmless. Each social group is a different unit. Each group differs from other groups, sometimes by reason of what we are compelled to call racial differences, in other cases by reason of different factors in past history or in present circumstances—differences of environment (**27**). We may seem to be in as difficult a position as the schoolboy when asked to find out the sum of three oranges, two apples and five plums on the plea that they are fruit and are all sold at one and the same shop. Fundamentals come first. The elements must be separated out and then only can we constitute our unities. There are elements common to all human groups, high or low, Western or Eastern. All are made up of men and women. All need food. All get their food from the bounty of nature. For the raw material of food, clothing, shelter and implements all depend on natural products. All the mature individuals in a group have passed through a period, which may be very prolonged, of dependence on others for their sustenance and nurture. Men and women, high and low, by reason of their sex differences, have different functions. The sex division is natural, inevitable, universal. The problems which the conditions of this struggle with and within nature engender are fundamentally identical for us all. But that very fundamental identity is often obscured by the differences in the standpoint from which the problems are viewed at different levels of culture. Therefore in examining and classifying our material, it is permissible to consider how any problem has been or can be stated for and by any social group, how many solutions of such problems are possible for any group with due regard to the mental powers of that group and its technical abilities and its resources as provided by its physical environment. Then we may endeavour to ascertain why any particular solution of a given problem was preferred, what factors decided the preference. Convergence, diffusion by borrowing, independent invention, centralisation round a common core. Such are the theories of origins. It is not an easy task, and no very certain results can be assured, since the complexity of Indian culture is great, even in the lower levels. *Le vrai primitif* exists nowhere. What we find is a number of groups who rank in material things with very lowly people, who yet have invented systems of religion, complex and ingenious systems, so that the intellectual development ranges to the highest fancies of fine philosophy. We shall find our material among the folk that dwell in the jungles and inaccessible hills of the continent, among that welter of tribes who nestle among the hills of Assam and Burma up to the Himalayas, yielding evidence of their lowly culture in the simple and elementary economic organisation, in the characteristics of their speech as well as in the strength and persistence of sentiments which enwrap their lives in a close mantle of custom. Some are timid and feeble folk, remnants it may be of what were once strong-tribes. Others are mighty warriors, quick to revenge. All have a long, unwritten history behind them. Few, if indeed any, are in any real sense the original inhabitants of the secluded spots where they now dwell. They may teach us something of the mental development of human society, for among them are preserved in full vitality modes of thought in sharpest contrast with the spirit of science which seeks " by the constant interrogation of physical and social facts, to penetrate the secret laws which govern them " (28).

1a. Rivers, *Dreams and Primitive Culture*, p. 24.
2. Rivers, *op. cit.*, p. 25.
3. *Naga Tribes of Manipur*, p. 129.
3a. Man, E. H., *The Andaman Islanders*. pp. 28, 29
3b. Hutton, *Sema Nagas*, p. 231, 246.
4. Hahn, *Einführung in das Gebiet der Kols-Mission*, p. 116.
5. Rivers, *op. cit.*, p. 5.
6. Rivers, *Instinct and the Unconscious*, p. 230.
7. Rivers, *Dreams and Primitive Culture*, p. 25.
8. Lang, *Anthropological Essays presented to (Sir) E. B. Taylor*, p. 211.
9. McDougall, *The Group Mind*, p. 11, p. 209 sq., *cf.* Ellen Semple. Influence of Geographical Environment—*passim*.
10. Rivers, *Instinct and the Unconscious*, p. 18.
11. Rivers, *Festskrift Tillagrad Edvard Westermarck*.
11a. *Naga Tribes of Manipur*, p. 47.
11b. *Naga Tribes of Manipur*, p. 182.
12. McDougall, *op. cit.* p. 117.
13. Keith, *Engines of the Human Body*, p. 235.
13a. *The Lushei Kuki Clans*, p. 102.
13b. *The Sema Nagas*, p. 205.
14. *Cf.* Durkheim, *Méthode Sociologique*, p. 10, *passim*.

15. Report on the Condition of the Sonthals in the Districts of Birbhum, Bankura, Midnapore and Balasore, M. C. McAlpine, I.C.S., p. 13.

16. *Ibid.*, p. 76.

17. *Archiv für Religions-wissenschaft*, xii. 456.

17a. *Angami Nagas*, p. 396.

18. *L'Année Sociologique*, vol. ix., p. 1.

19. Payne, *History of the New World called America*, vol. ii, p. 103.

20. *Linguistic Survey of India*, vol. iii., part 1, p. 5 (characteristics of Tibeto-Burman Languages), vol. iv., p. 23 (characteristics of Munda languages).

21. *Ibid.*

22. See Rivers, *History of Melanesian Society*, vol. ii., p. 488 *sq.*

23. Rivers, *Dreams and Primitive Culture*, p. 24.

24. Haddon, *Folklore*, xxxi. p. 12.

24a. Sir Baldwin Spencer, Pres. Address Aust. Association, 1921, p. 30.

24b. Sir Arthur Keith, *Nationality and Race*, p. 9.

25. *Méthode Sociologique*, p. xv.

26. *Folklore as an Historical Science*, p. 171.

27. McDougall, *op. cit.*, p. 209.

28. Payne, *op. cit.*, vol. i., p. 277.

LECTURE II.

The Economic Life of the Lower Culture—Analysis of Motives, Religious and Other—Dominance of Group Life—Density and Conditions physical and political affecting density—Size of Social Groups—Food Quest and Materials—Jhum and Terraced Fields—Hunting Groups—Houses and Villages—Dress—Firemaking, Stone, Metal and Woodwork, Pottery.

I am confronted by certain difficulties in my approach to these studies of the economics of the lower culture. In the first place I shall disappoint the experts in the dismal science if they expect anything very startlingly new or immediately useful as an addition to their knowledge, because the " natural " mode of existence does not lend itself to any degree of elaborate organisation. In the next place I think it is very difficult—and for me impossible—to analyse the life of these communities as I know and regard them, into separate and distinct compartments. The play of purely economic forces is so closely intertwined with social forces of what we are in the habit of treating as a different order, that the whole must be regarded as a whole, not as a mechanical combination of so many independent parts. That considerations of an economic order do play a real even a large part in determining the behaviour of these societies of the lower culture, cannot be denied, and yet such is the power of tradition that the activity of economic forces is obscured and coloured often when most discernible, by the dominance of sentiments which a modern analytic mind would describe as religious. Then we come to the third of my difficulties, that arises from the notable fact that we are dealing with communities, not with individuals, so that whatever may be the verdict of the specialist in the controversy as to the nature, origin and function of the group mind, we are dealing with groups possessed of no inconsiderable social organisation and structure with a high degree of mental homogeneity, with relatively small spatial extent and therefore enabled to practise collective deliberation and to display collective volition in intense forms. It will be evident that to define the lower culture exclusively on psychological grounds as under the thraldom of tradition would now enable me to include many groups in my survey which I therefore propose to limit by adding thereto an economic element derived from their relations to other communities, for the special reason that we have in India an economic organisation of social units which is based on a definite scale of precedence according to economic occupation, such that, though at any one moment it may appear immobile and rigid, yet on a wide view it appears to possess a degree of elasticity and local variation, according to differences of economic pressure. The groups of the lower culture stand with but few exceptions apart from this organisation which is the Hindu polity. Therefore economic independence of this polity, which varies in degrees as we shall see, and in respect to certain specified commodities, may be taken as a distinguishing feature of the lower culture.

It will therefore serve our purpose if we investigate the lower culture and its economics by examining typical cases as to their food supplies and the methods of preparing them, as to the materials and methods used in the preparation of shelter from the weather, and the clothes they wear, to observe whence and how they obtain, and how they work, metals, with special note of instances where by reason of the development of natural resources special local industries have sprung into being, which necessitate some—albeit rudimentary—organisation for transport and distribution.

Attention must be given to the size of the groups classified as belonging to the lower culture, in order to ascertain whether and how far we "accept the general principle that, on the whole and in the long run during the earlier stages of human evolution, the complexity and coherence of the social order follow upon the size of the group; which, since its size in turn follows upon the mode of the economic life, may be described as the food-group" (**1**).

DENSITY.

Analysis of the facts recorded at the 1911 census (**2**) shows that one-eleventh of the population is supported by two-fifths of the total area of the Indian Empire; that one-eleventh of the total area supports one-third of the population; that the density ranges from one per square mile in Chagai in Baluchistan to nearly 2,000 per square mile in part of the Dacca district; that density of population in India is dependent on the sum total of agricultural conditions in which are to be included the area under cultivation, rainfall, physical configuration, while the effect of variations consequent on the nature of the soil is difficult if not impossible of distinction and separation from the general mass of agricultural phenomena.(**3**) The complexity of these phenomena is increased by the obvious fact that the conditions prior to, as well as those which are directly attributable to the "Pax Britannica," exercise an effect on the social life in this aspect of the 300 millions of human beings then enumerated. There is evidence which leads to the conclusion that as minute investigations showed was the case in Bihar in 1901, the tracts which can support most people are those where rice is grown (**4**). As I see the question, it may be put thus—what is the density of population which (subject to any special exceptions) can be fairly regarded as an indication of conditions, social, physical and historical, unfavourable to the development of economic organisation to a stage distinctly higher than that of the simple tribal form? Is a density of 50 per square mile too high when the average all over India is taken as 175 per square mile? Is a density of 25 per square mile unfairly low ? The Hills Division of Assam has 34 to the square mile, but in the Lushai Hills we drop to 13 per square mile. In Baluchistan, a land of contradictions and contrasts, we get to six per square mile. In parts of Chota Nagpur we have 38 to the square mile, and in Burma as a result of the great dissimilarities of surface conditions, of recent political conditions and of the characters of the inhabitants, there are areas with only 15 to the square mile ; others with 38 and with 23, despite certain advantages which are nullified by the physical conditions, and areas where the population is over 120 to the square mile. Parts of the Central Provinces are but sparsely populated, and in the view of those who know the country the determining factor is to be found in the physical characteristics of the country and in its past history. In Madras there are but few areas which fall below the general average. The Agency tracts in the north, physically conterminous with the Chota Nagpur area, consist of forest-clad ranges, inhabited by improvident and ignorant aboriginal tribes such as the Khond, "a short, thick-set good-humoured jungle man. He lives in a cabin built of rough hewn planks, has a predilection for toddy and an aversion for education : generally speaks the truth, worships singularly unpleasant devils in a strangely unpleasant manner, and in his worldly affairs exhibits a deplorable but eminently cheerful disregard for the morrow" (5). When we touch on the hills, wherein abide the Todas (6) worshippers of the sacred dairy and its buffaloes, the Badagas, the Kurumbas the Irulas and the Kotas,(7) we come again on an area where the population is relatively sparse, and exhibits features which enable it to be assigned to the lower culture. Still further south the high ranges in the Devikulam Taluk of the prosperous State of Travancore (7), which seem once to have been held by a people of relatively high culture, are now inhabited by wandering folk, as is demonstrated by the low density of 55 per square mile.

SIZE OF SOCIAL GROUPS.

More significant, especially when regarded in association with the general distribution of culture, is the size of the social groups. We have seen groups as small as those of the Khereya, who move from jungle to jungle not more than one or two families at a time(**8**). The Birhors wander about in small groups of from two to about ten families, stop and hunt in one place for about a week or a fortnight and then move on to another jungle until they come back to their original starting point" (**9**). The Irulas in South Arcot "dwell in scattered huts never more than two or three in one place —which are little round thatched hovels with a low doorway through which one can just crawl, built among the fields" (**10**). The Kadirs of Cochin live in groups of from ten to fifteen or twenty huts, usually built of bamboo, close to water, or in an open glade of the forest. These settlements are rarely permanent, yet "it is wonderful to see the ingenuity of these people whose wants are few and whose life is very simple. Their requirements are, in fact, satisfied with the materials available in the vicinity of their abodes" (**11**). We cannot hesitate to classify these people as belonging to the lower culture. A further stage of social and economic development has been reached by the tribes inhabiting the hills of Assam. There are large villages with 5,000 or 6,000 inhabitants, yet there are also tiny settlements in the jungles of from four to five huts, built with ingenuity and skill of bamboo and cane, in which dwell Kukis, nomad agriculturists. "The peculiar vagabond strain," says Colonel Shakespear, "in the blood of the Kuki Lushei race, if not controlled, leads to villages splitting into hamlets and hamlets subdividing till in the Manipur Hills we find single houses in the midst of dense jungle, several miles from the next habitation". (**12**). The Pax Britannica has removed the need of forming large communities for the purposes of defence.

Not only have we to take count of the dominance of the bamboo, but some weight must also be assigned in our explanation of the "peculiar vagabond strain" of the Kuki Lushei race to the custom by which "Each son of a chief, as he attained a marriageable age, was provided with a wife at his father's expense and given a certain number of households from his father's village and sent forth to a village of his own. Henceforth he ruled as an independent chief and his success or failure depended on his own talents for ruling. He paid no tribute to his father, but was expected to help him in his quarrels with neighbouring chiefs, but when fathers lived long, it was not unusual to find their sons disowning even this amount of subordination. The youngest son remained in his father's village and succeeded not only to the village but also to all the property" (**13**). There are traces of this custom which still lingers among us under the name of Borough English, in the more settled communities of the Hills, and one large Naga group, the Semas, contrary to the usual Naga order, has hereditary chiefs, "the elder sons becoming chiefs in their own villages during the fathers' lifetime, provided the sons are able to found separate villages, and one of the younger sons probably succeeding in his father's village" (**14**). Economic conditions engender social habits which persist as customs long after the original conditions have been modified or ceased to affect them actively. The effect of political conditions upon the social life is especially marked here. In 1911 it was observed that "The decrease in the size of villages had led to an important modification of the custom under which the youngest son inherits his father's village and property. The *raison d'être* of this system of inheritance is that elder sons established villages of their own on their marriage. In order to enable them to do so a certain number of headmen or Upas and also of the common people were told off to accompany the young chief and form the nucleus of his new village. When all the elder sons had been established in this way, it is not unnatural that the youngest should inherit his father's village and property, and on him rested the responsibility for his mother's support. But while there has been no tendency for chiefs' families to decrease, the average size of villages has been decreased by half, and there are not enough houses to go round among the sons. Indeed, in some cases none of the sons have been able to start a separate village, and it is obvious that under these circumstances inheritance should pass to the eldest son and this change has been readily accepted by the people" (**15**).

FOOD-QUEST.

It is no far cry from the teeming streets of Calcutta to the jungles of Bankura, wherein dwell the Khereyas, whose mode of life is simplicity itself. They make very small huts with the branches of trees thatching them with leaves and using creepers as ropes. They lie down on the bare ground and never use coat or wrapper even in winter. Their most favourite and common food is the boiled roots of creepers, with rice once a day when available. Fire they know and make by friction. Only one or two families live in one jungle, and when the family grows some of them remove to a new jungle. Yet their women are skilful in making very fine mattresses which they sell, but never use; they know how to sharpen their digging shovels by fire, and work simple leaf bellows (**16**). Rai Bahadur Sarat Chandra Roy, to whom the science of Indian anthropology owes a great debt, tells us of the Birhors, a jungle folk of Hazaribagh, who have made no progress in fifty years, or none since the days of that great pioneer, Colonel Dalton. They still wander through the jungles in quest of food in small groups of from three to ten families, live in mere improvised leaf sheds and subsist on yams, honey, tubers of various kinds, and on the varied produce of the mahua tree. Some settle down, but slender and weak are the ties which fasten them to agriculture. Some revert to the wandering life in the jungle from sheer *ennui*, others take easy fright and at the slightest ill-treatment, real or fancied, fall back to their old nomad life. Where they do cultivate, it is by burning the jungle, scratching the soil and sowing beans and maize (**17**). From the same gifted inquirer we learn of the Pahiras, a folk who have now adopted a patois of Bengali as their language, that even to this day most Pahiras have to depend mainly on yams and edible roots and fruits and the corolla of the mahua (*Bassia latifolia*) which their women gather in the jungles, with some variety from the humble gains of the chase and occasional fishing. To such insects and grubs come not amiss. Simple as is their dress at its best, there are still those who have to wear creeper bark, and there are current traditions of the days not so distant when all wore leaf or bark cloths (**18**). The bounty of the jungle provides sustenance for the dark-skinned, broad-nosed, short-statured inhabitants of the hills from the Nallamalai range to the Niligiris and on to the hills of Travancore State to Cape Comorin. In them, beyond a doubt, we have specimens of a race which we may call pre-Dravidian, and so avoid any attempt at assigning these interesting peoples to any family of races.

Set in the path of the monsoon and clothed with dense and lofty forests which generally are filled with evergreen trees covered all over with climbers diversified with patches of deciduous forest, the Andaman Islands are inhabited by a short-statured folk, whose smooth, greasy, satiny skin is an intense black in colour, like a black-leaded stove, whose hair, sooty-black or yellowish-brown in general appearance, grows in small rings on the head, which give it the appearance of growing in tufts. Such is the variety of the yield of forest and sea, whose harvest is never done, that though habitually heavy eaters, they never starve, since they find sustenance in fish, pork, turtle, iguana, wild cat, shellfish, larvae and fruit seeds, roots and honey. Yet when we first went there they did not know how to make fire and showed much skill in so carrying smouldering logs with them by land or sea that they were not extinguished **(19)**.

In the settled historic South, where Government recognises the rights of the forest tribes to collect and live by the produce of the forests, there are yet folk like the Irulas, whose dietary consists of "roots, wild fruits and honey," which they gather by "letting themselves down the face of the cliffs at night by ladders made of twisted creepers, who **(20)** always reject cooked rice, even when gratuitously offered." But little above them are the Chenchus **(21)**, in the hills of the Kurnool and Nellore districts, the Kadirs **(22)** of the Animalai hills who like the Veda Malars of Travancore file their teeth, whose women distend the lobes of their ears by massive earrings. When a Kadir collects wild honey, he will only do so while his wife or son watches above to prevent any foul play. They have a superstition that they should always return by the way they go down and decline to get to the bottom of the cliff, although the distance may be less and the work of reclimbing avoided. Mr. (now Sir) J. D. Rees, describing the collection of honey by the Kadirs of the southern hills, says that they "descend giddy precipices at night, torch in hand, to smoke out the bees and take away the honey. A stout creeper is suspended over the abyss, and it is established law of the jungle that no brother shall assist in holding it" **(23)**.

How, when, where, and in what circumstances agriculture had its origin, are questions on which I fear I can throw no light. As I see it, agriculture in the lower culture is not a simple business. It is a complex of many elements, sacrifices, tabus, dances, as well as sowing and weeding. It is the association of these elements, not any single element in the complex, that for the lower culture produces the results. Hence, as it seems to me, we must look for origins in the complex association of the various component elements, the human sacrifice, since we have folk like the Was (**24**) and Nagas (**25**) or the Khonds (**26**) who needed or thought they needed to begin the cultivation with the death of some human being, tabus of a long and oppressive nature, since to the Naga all minor activities are forbidden while the seed is in the soil and the harvest uncut (**27**).

A step towards better conditions in the food quest was taken when the simple form of jhum cultivation was introduced : " A tract is cleared by fire, cultivated for a year or two and then abandoned for another tract, where a like process is pursued. Known as Jhum on the North-East Frontier. This is the Kumari of South-West India, the Toungyan of Burma, the dahya of North India. Ponam, or ponacaud of Malabar. In the Philippine Islands it is known as guinges ; it is practised in the Ardennes under the name of sartage and in Sweden under the name of swedjande " (**28**). It is described by the historian of the New World called America as " the primitive mode of agriculture all over the world and widely practised even yet where virgin forest is abundant, for in such circumstances it is the most economical method becauses it promises the largest net return" (**29**).

Alongside of it, in many areas supplementing it, supplanting it, and independent of it, is the system of terraced fields, which are found in Europe, in England, Scotland, Wales and Ireland, (**30**) as well as in Arabia (**31**) and America (**32**). In Manipur, indeed, in one small area, we have " tribes who migrate periodically and practise only the jhum system of cultivation. We have tribes such as the Kabuis (and possibly the Marrings) who keep to the village sites with tenacity, but are compelled to change the area of their cultivation year by year in set rotation. They preserve the memory of other days by taking omens annually to decide the direction in which the cultivation is to be. We have large villages with extensive terraced fields magnificently irrigated with water brought from considerable distances in channels so well aligned that every advantage is taken of any natural slope encountered and awkward corners avoided or turned with admirable ingenuity. But this method of cultivation is not practicable everywhere, and fortunate are the tribes who occupy hills whose declivity is not too steep for such fields. By means of long and assiduous labour a field can be built up and provided with water so that large terraces represent the expenditure of a vast amount of energy and farming ability as well as much practical engineering skill." I have observed, too, that " when felling the jungle for the jhums it is usual to leave one tree in the middle of the field as a refuge for the tree spirit. Indeed, the scorched, scarred, twisted horror of some of these solitary stumps is enough to account for the belief that some spirit has chosen them as an abode. It is interesting to note the skill with which advantage is taken of the tree logs to employ them as retaining walls to keep the moisture in the ground thus making use of the principle of the terraced field in places where terraced fields are impossible on a large scale." Colonel McCulloch remarks that " Across the fields in parallel lines at no great distance apart they lay the unconsumed trunks of the trees ; these serve as dams to rains and preventives to the soil being carried away with it. In bamboo jungle the bamboo stumps serve the same purpose " (**33**). In the Khasia Hills " Forest lands are cleared by the process known as jhuming, the trees being felled early in the winter and allowed to lie till January or February when fire is applied, logs of wood being placed at intervals of a few feet to prevent, as far as possible, the ashes being blown away by the wind " (**34**). Exceptional interest attaches to this ingenious method of building up or scarping out the hillside to form terraced fields since they are found all over the world in frequent—but not universal—association with cultural features such as the erection of stone monuments, sun worship, and the search for wealth, as discussed at length and in careful exposition by Mr. Perry (**35**). Clearly this is a world problem, and local explanations are of little value. Negative as well as positive evidence has yet to be discussed and its meaning evaluated. The real significance of the frequent but not universal association of jhum cultivation with terraced fields has to be explained. So far as Assam is concerned we now know that people like the Semas, when urged by the Administration to follow the terrace system stated that "they were unable to do so as they did not know the sacrifices for terrace cultivation" (**36**). The plough is never used; yet in Manipur they see it in use. Here we have a light thrown suddenly on the minds of the lower culture. Unless the ritual proper to terraced fields is known, it is useless to make the experiment. The sacrifice is part, an integral essential part of the process. When the stars in their courses fight for the old order, not much that is new can be introduced. From the Sema country comes the information that "The heavy rain in **1918**, which ruined the millet crop, was put down in Shevekhe village to the irrigation channels dug by a pestilential innovator who wanted to make terraced fields instead of jhuming them like his forebears. The wrathful villagers broke them up" (**37**). The village Tory muttered "I told you so."

I may compare and contrast this recent evidence from the Naga Hills with an experience which I had in a Tangkhul Naga village in Manipur, where I saw a girl whom I had seen the year before in her native village where she was reputed to be a most skilful weaver of cloth. I asked her if she made any cloths of late, and was told that the new village into which she had married in the interval, would not let her make cloths. I asked the village headman why this useful craft was forbidden, and was told that they feared that if they let her do work which was right and proper in the village of her birth, they would draw down on them the magic of the other village. Infringement of the patent meant trouble somehow. While we may admire the skill and ingenuity of people in the lower culture who build up these wonderful terraced fields, we may ask ourselves whether they understand the process of germination as we do. They have not been brought up on the Epistle of St. Paul to the Corinthians, which might make this mystery as clear to them as it makes other mysteries clear to us. May we regard their position as this? "We have sown the seed, we have killed the fowls, as is right. In the old days we should have carried a human head round the fields. We have danced the dances, observed the prescribed tabus, gone through the whole ritual as ordained by custom, that is as it was performed by our ancestors who live again in our bodies. Because we have done all these things duly and in order, because each item of the long ritual is, or appears to be, as necessary as any other item in the complex of associated rites, because no item can be omitted, therefore we get the harvest, sometimes tenfold, sometimes fivefold, and sometimes we get no harvest at all." If to this argument the suggestion were made that experiment might be made to see whether any item could be safely left out or modified, the answer would be obvious—"Why worry when the known recognised, approved, established methods give all the results desired? Why run the risk of failure? Why run the risk of the magic of the other people whose secret we are asked to imitate? Yet they use matches when they can get them because, as I presume, matches have the prestige of an admittedly superior culture behind them. What comes from people whom they know and regard as at best their equals, more often as their inferiors, has no prestige, is not imitated. What comes to them from a strange culture, regarded as superior and to be imitated, may have prestige partly because it comes from a superior culture or even because it comes from a culture recognised as different to their own. The reasons why this custom is chosen for imitation and that rejected can seldom be ascertained exactly and definitely. The lower culture is what it is because it imposes these restrictions upon itself, because it is illiberal of naturalisation of new ideas, because it is ruled by custom.

Nor are the conquests won by trouble and difficulty always retained. The force of ancient custom may be too strong, as the Government of India found when trying to cure criminal tribes like the Maghaya Doms (**38**) by settling them in agricultural communities. The Dom is still a nomad. The settlements, we learn, served as houses for the women and children, but the men were seldom to be found in them. The Baigas were forbidden to practise the ancient jhum method of cultivation and "attempts made to train them to regular cultivation . . . in some villages the Baiga cultivators, if left unwatched, would dig up the grain which they themselves had sown as seed in their fields and eat it" (**39**).

Agriculture is not in the lower culture a simple business. Sacrifices have to be offered up, ritual of a long and complex nature has to be performed. All the items are important. None may be omitted. It is a complex of many factors, each of which has validity. Therefore its origins must be sought in a complex of ideas which exhibits the growth and history of the association of the several elements we now perceive in combination. Conditions in India, as far as the typical practices of the lower culture are concerned, do not now afford us much help in our quest for origins.

In earlier days, no doubt, there were many folk, like the Chenchus who lived in caves; even now, here and there, are those who use caves as places of temporary habitation (**40**). In general, the people use and construct habitations which are of various degrees of simplicity. The Yanadis, who inhabit the Telugu area, a dark-skinned broad-nosed people, " live in low conical huts rudely built of bamboo and palmyra leaves, grass or millet stalks, with a small entrance, through which grown up people have to creep (**41**). In a tanda or settlement of the migratory Birhors the huts are mere improvised leaf-sheds in the form of low triangular kumbas or straw shelters such as their neighbours the Mundas and the Oraons erect near their rice fields. Each family erects its separate shed or sheds made of branches and leaves. Each of these sheds has one opening, sometimes provided with a door made of branches and leaves (**42**). Why build more elaborately when in a week or so there will be a move on to another jungle ? When we come to the mountain ranges of Assam, where as we have seen there are in these days tiny hamlets or even solitary huts in the midst of jungle as there are also large well-built villages, there is still a measure of simplicity discernible in the range of material as well as in the methods of construction. In the Naga villages are solid houses with plank walls and roofs of heavy thatch. In the jungle the nomad Kuki builds lightly and a habitation of sorts can be erected in a few hours with bamboo mats as walls and with leaves to thatch and keep out the rain. The relaxation of the pressure which kept instinctive nomads like the Lusheis together, has, as we have noted, allowed freer play to the tendency to dispersion, and with that goes a diminution of the architectural skill. The construction of the large solidly-built houses involves co-operation, provision of material as well as technical skill. Hence there may be a lessening of these valuable qualities as a result of the weakening of the bonds which drove these people to form large units.

Intensity of social life seems to go with increase in the size of the social unit and then to diminish by a sort of decreasing return due, perhaps, to difficulties of maintaining communications throughout the unit. Diminution of external pressure may also promote disintegration.

One feature of the domestic architecture of the lower culture will require attention, not from its interest as evincing skill in the use of material, but as the most important means of preserving social life. Among the Andamanese (**43**), among groups such as the Nagas, Lushais, Munda-speaking people of Chota Nagpur, Dravidian tribes of Southern and Central India, Gonds, Khonds, Kurumbas, and in many parts of the world, is found the institution of the Bachelors' Hall where the young men of the community sleep and live. It is often more pretentious architecturally than private dwelling places, and from that point of view, notable. Its absence in the case of small jungle tribes is an indication of the development of their resources, material as well as mental. Nomadism affords no possibility of the development of an institution such as this, and their circumstances compel them to Nomadism.

DRESS.

Such folk as the Andamanese exhibit local variations in the matter of dress, for while Jarawas go naked, others wear a bunch of leaves, or a loose tassel of narrow strips of bark, or a bunching tassel of fibre (**44**). " No clothing as we understand the word, is worn by either sex ; there are, however, certain so-called ornamental circlets, garters, bracelets, cinctures, and necklaces of bones, wood, or shell, which are its substitute and serve to remove in some measure the impression that they are naked ; these appendages are not worn as symbols of rank or (if we except the ro-gun) of status, and their manufacture devolves always on the females of the community " (**45**). Absence of clothing as a means of protection against the climate may be intelligible enough in these Islands, where the lowest temperature recorded is 63 and the mean temperature is not less than 70. But in the hills of Assam climatic conditions are different, yet even now (**46**) there are naked folk. With them as with others

(**47**) a cloth is worn when there are strangers about. As typical of the level which has been classified as the figleaf state of society, there are, as Thurston remarks (**48**) some tribes in Southern India who have only recently advanced beyond that state. There are others who are still to be found in that state. The Thanda Pulayans, of Cochin (**49**) are so called from the thanda garment worn by their females. Thanda is a waterplant (*isolepis articulata Nees*) the leaves of which are cut into lengths of 2 feet, woven at one end and tied round their waist in such a manner that the strings unwoven hang loosely round the loins up to the knees." Colonel Dalton records with sombre humour how the Juang girls sat silent in his tent while he discussed customs and religion with the men of the party, till, to his horror, he saw the ladies who " sat nestled in a corner . . . were dropping great tears . . . like dew-drops on the green leaves. Tenderly seeking the cause of their distress he learned that the leaves of their attire were becoming dry, stiff and uncomfortable, and if they were not allowed to go to the woods for a change, the consequences would be serious." (**50**). The adoption of cloth by the Juangs was brought about by the persuasive power of Captain, afterwards Major-General Sir James Johnstone, whose *Experiences in Manipur and the Naga Hills* form an interesting volume. Among the Padam Abors, on the banks of the Dibong River ;" All females with pretensions to youth wear suspended in front from a string round the loins a row of from three to a dozen shell-shaped embossed plates of bell metal from about six to three inches in diameter, the largest in the middle, the others gradually diminishing in size as they approach the hips. These plates rattle and chink as they move like prisoners' chains. Very young girls except for warmth wear nothing but these appendages but the smallest of the sex is never seen without them, and even adult females are often seen with no other covering" (**51**). The

Ghyghasi-Miris, a poor, meanly-clad, badly-fed, ill-looking people of stunted growth, living in small villages of ten or a dozen houses, built closely together in some position difficult of access, deem their women dressed when wearing only a small petticoat made of filaments of cane woven together, about a foot in breadth and fastened tightly round the loins (**52**.)

From the *sancta simplicitas* of " dress " of this kind I turn to the elaborate costume of an Angami warrior, whose prowess in war and in love, whose status in society can be determined accurately by the distinctions of his dress—distinctions as important to him as the " Third pip " to some of us a few years ago. Kilt and tail and cloth and sporran, if I may call it so, are not left to individual choice. Each has a social value, a meaning and a significance (**53**).

FIRE-MAKING.

That curious creature, Neanderthal man—whose massive brows, receding chin, big brain, thick neck, loose-limbed with an easy, shuffling gait, make him still an interesting study from the history of the physical evolution of mankind—was skilled as a flint-worker, " had fire at his command and buried his dead " (**54**). Thus as far back as the mid-Pleistocene Age, there was in the world a race of human beings using fire. I know of no tribe which is completely ignorant of fire. (**55**). The Andamanese " like the quondam aborigines of Tasmania have always been ignorant of the art of producing fire, they naturally display much care and skill in the measures they adopt for avoiding such inconvenience as might be caused by the extinction of their fires. When they all leave an encampment with the intention of returning in a few days, besides taking with them one or more smouldering logs wrapped in leaves if the weather be wet, they place a large burning log or faggot in some sheltered spot where, owing to the character and condition of the wood invariably selected, it smoulders for several days, and can be rekindled when required" (56). The production of fire by friction is still practised in two forms by many peoples in India. Indeed, the most sacred fire of Brahmanic Hinduism, the Homa, is produced by this means (57). "In making fire by friction, the Kotas of the Nilgiris employ three forms of apparatus: (1) a vertical and horizontal stick with sockets and grooves, both made of twigs of *Rhodomyrtus tomentosus*; (2) a small piece of the root of *Salix tetrasperma* is spliced into a stick, which is rotated in a socket in a piece of the root of the same tree; (3) a small piece of the root of this tree made tapering at each end with a knife or fragment of bottle glass, is firmly fixed in the wooden handle of a drill. A shallow cavity and groove are made in a block of the same wood, and a few crystalline particles from the ground are dropped into the cavity" (58). The sawing method is employed by such people as the Paniyans and Vizagapatam hillmen, who take a piece of dry bamboo, split lengthways, and make a notch in the convex side. A knife edge is then cut on a piece of tamarind wood, shaped to fit the notch. A piece of cloth is laid below the notched bamboo, across which, in the notch, the tamarind wood is drawn violently till dust drops on to the cloth below, till smoke, and finally flame, appears in the cloth (59). The flint and steel are used by the Kadirs (60) and the Irulas (61). It is recorded that "though the Badagas make fire by friction, reference is made in their folk legends, not to this mode of obtaining fire, but to *chakkamukhi* (flint and steel), which is repeatedly referred to in connection with cremation" (62). Are we to suspect that the use of flint and steel has been superseded by the frictional method, except in the solemnity of funeral rites, preserved there by reason of its associations? Iron, we know from the same authority (63), is carried by the son or representative of the deceased as having a "repulsive power over the spirits that hover about the dead." It may be that iron, a new, strange, powerful material—is used for its novelty, just as with the Lusheis the hunter who kills a rhinoceros can escape the penalty of his success by going to the forge while the corpse of a man who has died by accident or by wild animals, if brought into the village at all, which is forbidden in some cases, is "deposited in the forge" (**64**). Among the Semas it is also advisable to sit on a dao because iron breaks all gennas, the evil effect of the forbidden act being neutralised by the iron of the dao (**65**).

Perhaps the most interesting method of firemaking is that by means of the fire piston whose use "extends sporadically over a wide area, from Northern Burma and Siam through the Malay Peninsula and the Malayan Archipelago to its eastern limits in the islands of Luzon and Mindanao in the Philippines" (**66**). As Sir Edward Tylor observed (**67**) "There is a well-known scientific toy made to show that heat is generated by compression of air. It consists of a brass tube closed at one end into which a packed piston is sharply forced down, thus igniting a piece of tinder within the tube. It is curious to find an apparatus on this principle (made in ivory, hard wood, etc.) used as a practical means of making fire in Burmah, and even among the Malays." Mr. Henry Balfour, in summarising the evidence, shows that the fire piston was discovered in France in 1802, that it was patented in England in 1807, and was sold in a pocket form by tobacconists in Paris. As he remarks, "The problem is to ascertain whether this peculiar and very specialised method of fire-production was introduced into the oriental regions from Europe, or whether it was invented independently by the little civilized peoples among whom it is found as an appliance of practical everyday use" (**68**). No very definite conclusion is formulated, perhaps *ex abundanti cautela*, though in answer to the objection that "It seems almost incredible that so delicate and far from obvious a method can have been discovered whether by accident or by gradual development by any of the eastern peoples amongst whom it has been found in use " our authority recognises that " There is no inherent impossibility in such a double origin, cases of independent invention of similar appliances in widely separated regions having frequently arisen, and " there is no record of introduction by Europeans " (**69**). The impossibilities of yesterday are the certainties of tomorrow, and while, beyond a doubt, there has been much transmission of culture, without which it is impossible to explain the complexity of existing cultures, I myself am convinced that the extreme advocates of the " transmission of culture " tend to overstrain a good case, laying down, as a law without exceptions that in no case—be the merits or the circumstances ever so clear—may we admit the possibility of independent origins, of convergence or even of singular solutions.

In the lower, as in the higher culture, the raw materials used by man in satisfaction of his various needs are the products of either the animal or the vegetable or the mineral kingdom. They may be used in the condition in which they are found. They may be used after being subjected to processes controlled by man which range in order of complexity from the application of fire (involving a knowledge of means of making fire) to the combination of long complicated chemical processes in the course of which use is made of methods and knowledge derived from many—often very distinct—sources. These methods, this knowledge, can be traced back in many cases and dated, chronologically. Even the simple processes—the direct processes—involve a knowledge which is not immediately given, but can be won only by observation, of the properties of the materials yielded by these three sources. I believe that " In the early stages of culture progress, the stones employed as implements and in the manufacture of implements and other articles, as well also as building stone, were gathered at random wherever they happened to be found on the surface of the ground" (**70**). The practices of living races may give evidence of the methods and processes employed in the past, as, for instance, that just as in the lower culture men bury food with their dead, because they think the spirit of the dead will need food, so in the distant Palaeolithic age when men buried food with their dead, it was because in those remote days they too believed that the dead man had a spirit, and that it needed and could get benefit from food. I will not now discuss the assumptions which underlie this attitude. In dealing with cultural data it is possible to classify the facts according to the degree of elaboration to which knowledge based on and derived from observation, is used in producing which is needed and desired, from the raw materials as found in nature.

The Andamanese use cyrena shells and quartz flakes as cutting instruments and "the more distant tribes still retain the use with scarcely any modification of most of the stone and other implements which served their ancestors" (**71**) but "maintain that they never, even when iron was scarce, made arrowheads, axes, or adzes or chisels, of stone" (**72**). They are now aware of the superiority of iron over stone and work pieces of hoop-iron, keel-plate, etc., cold, without application of heat, by simple hammering and grindery on stone anvils and whetstones, with stone hammers, by the processes which were, and are, used to make stone implements. In many parts of the peninsula stone implements are occasionally found, and are commonly regarded as thunderbolts and as endowed with magical qualities (**73**). Copper implements have been found in the Central Provinces, the Gangetic Valley, and in Burma, where both they and stone weapons are said to be thunderbolts. (**75**). Such tribes as the Semas use regularly a hoe "made of a piece of pliant wood or bamboo bent into the form of a horseshoe, with the ends prolonged to cross one another, which Mr.

Hutton considers may be the prototypes of iron hoes of the same shape used by some of the Lhotas and many of the Ao and Konyaks (**74**). The truth is that wooden as well as stone implements are used largely by tribes who use iron implements and know how to use fire to work iron. From elsewhere, from America (**75a**) comes the proof of the extraordinary culture in matters of technique that may be reached by people ignorant of metal tools and examination of the products of the lower culture in any good museum will reveal the excellence of the products of what not unfairly may be called the wooden age as distinct from the stone age.

When Colonel Dalton made the acquaintance of the Juangs, he found them with "no knowledge whatever of metals. They have no iron smiths nor smelters of iron. They have no word in their own language for iron or other metals. They neither spin nor weave nor have they ever attained to the simplest knowledge of pottery."

(**76**) In the vocabularies collected for the *Linguistic Survey of India* the word for iron in Juang is given as *luha*, a Hindu loan word (**77**). Yet it is symptomatic of Indian economic policy that iron workers are low down in the scale of precedence because "The iron industry is associated with the primitive tribes who furnished the whole of the metal prior to its importation from Europe" (**78**). Formerly a flourishing industry it has now sadly diminished, as in the Khasi Hills, owing partly to the competition of iron from England and partly to the denudation of the country of its timber so that charcoal can no longer be made (**79**). In the Chota Nagpur area—in the case of the less advanced groups such as the Kharias—the blacksmith is a member of the group, as he is among the Nagas and Lusheis. In larger communities such as the Mundas and Oraons, he is a village official and an outsider. The supplies of the metal (**63**) (generally in the shape of roughly-worked hoes) are obtained from sources outside. By this dependence on outside supplies some of these backward people come into contact with representatives of superior culture. Iron-smelting demands means to get the high temperature necessary, of devices for tempering and annealing the tools fashioned, and in some cases a knowledge of fluxes and reduction-agents, so that even though, as with the Angamis, the tools actually used by the blacksmith are stones, for anvils and hammers, split bamboos used as tongs and the double piston bellows, made of bamboo tubes and skin packing, the practical knowledge of metal working processes has reached a fair level (**80**).

The Andamanese make pots from a particular kind of clay, found only in a few places, where the work is carried on. Strips of kneaded clay from which all stones have been removed, are made by the fingers and palms. The cup-like base, round or sometimes pointed, is first shaped and then the pot is built up, one roll after another being added and pressed to the desired thinness. The vessel is scraped inside and out by a cyrena shell, and wavy, checked or striped designs engraved by means of a pointed stick. It is then placed in the sun or before a fire to dry, and care taken to harden all parts equally. It is then baked by placing burning pieces of wood both inside and around the vessel. The pots so made are of three sizes, the largest seen only in permanent encampments, a medium size which is almost invariably provided with a rough basket work casing, and a small size useful when occasion for a migration as for a death (**81**). I have seen pots made in circular form by a simple use of the bamboo as a core. " The clay is slightly damped and then rolled out on a board which is first powdered with fine grit to prevent the clay from adhering too closely. It is then coiled round a bamboo stem and the base of the vessel cut out. At first the shape is that of a plain cylinder. It is then moulded by hand into the curves required, and after a partial hardening in the sun is baked in a furnace outside the village. They make vessels of all sizes. These vessels are devoid of any but the simplest ornamentation" (**82**). Among the Angamis, "pots are only made in certain villages . . . where clay is available. They are modelled from the lump by hand, without the aid of any wheel or implements, roughly round, with a somewhat greater circumference near the base than at the mouth, the lip of which is turned outwards" (**83**).

Among the Lusheis (**84**) as with the Semas and other Naga tribes (**85**) only women make pots.

Wooden vessels, platters, cups, bamboo cylinders, buffalo horns, gourds, leaves, are used in the storage, preparation and consumption of food, and are all articles made from raw materials furnished by the immediate environment.

These localised and specialised industries such as pot-making, salt working, have a special economic importance since from these centres springs up trade by barter, with the subsequent development of special groups for the transportation to markets and distribution there of these products. It was to procure iron that the Jarawas made their long series of raids on the outlying parts of the Andaman settlement (**86**). It is to procure iron and salt that the Naga visits the plains (**87**). Peaceful penetration is effected by simple trade of this sort. The economic effect is to develop specialisation and differentiation of function—to lay the foundation of economic organisation—which is here presented in its simplest forms.

1. Marett, *Anthropology*, p. 159.
2. Census Report, 1911, vol. i., p. 13 *et seq.*
3. *Ibid.*, p. 26.
4. *Ibid.*, p. 29.
5. Census Report, 1911, vol. xii., p. 6.
6. *Ibid.*, p. 16.
7. Census Report, 1911, vol. xxiii., pp. 22–26.
8. Report on the condition of the Santals, p. 67.
9. *Journal of the Bihar and Orissa Research Society*, Dec., 1916, p. 3.
10. *Castes and Tribes of Southern India*, ii. 389.
11. *Cochin Tribes and Castes*, i. 3, 4.

12. *The Lushei Kuki Clans*, p. 21.
13. *Ibid.*, p. 43.
14. Hutton, *The Angami Nagas*, p. 358.
15. Census Report, 1911, vol. iii., p. 138.
16. Report on the Condition of the Santals, pp. 66, 67.
17. *Journal of the Bihar and Orissa Research Society*, December, 1916, pp. 1–11.
18. *Journal of the Bihar and Orissa Research Society*, December, 1920, p. 527–539.
19. Census Report, 1901, vol. iii., pp. 47–67.
20. *Castes and Tribes of S. India*, ii., 383, 389.
21. *Ibid.*, p. 26 *et seq.*
22. *Castes and Tribes of S. India*, iii., 6 *et seq.*
23. *Ibid.*, p. 14.
24. *Gazetteer of Upper Burma*, vol. i., part 1, p. 497 *et seq.*
25. Hutton, *The Angami Nagas*, p. 161.
26. *Castes and Tribes of S. India*, vol. iii., p. 372 *et seq.*
27. *Naga Tribes of Manipur*, p. 166 *sq.*
28. Hobson Jobson, s.v. Jhum.
29. *History of the New World called America*, i. 333.
30. *The Village Community*, p. 75 *et seq.*
31. *Arabia Infelix*, p. 101 *sq.*, picture, p. 103.
32. *History of the New World called America*, i. 340.
33. *The Naga Tribes of Manipur*, p. 50 *et seq.*
34. *The Khasis*, p. 39.
35. *The Megalithic Culture of Indonesia*, *passim*. See also *The Semas*, p. 391 sq.
36. *Nature*, December 15, 1921, p. 512.
37. *The Sema Nagas*, p. 214 *n.*
38. *The Outcasts*, G. R. Clarke, I.C.S., p. 6.
39. *Tribes and Castes of the Central Provinces*, ii. 90.
40. *Castes and Tribes of S. India*, iv. 169. (Plate).
41. *Ibid.*, vii., p. 422 and p. 427.
42. *Journal of the Bihar and Orissa Research Society*, December, 1916, p. 5.
43. Census Report, 1901, p. 61.
44. *Ibid.*, p. 50.
45. Man, *The Andaman Islanders*, pp. 109, 110.
46. Hutton, *Angami Nagas*, p. 384–6.
47. *Ethnographic Notes in Southern India*, pp. 530–2.
48. *Ibid.*, p. 524, *cf.* Crooke in *J.R.A.I.*, xlix., 237 *et seq.*
49. *Cochin Tribes and Castes*, i. 89.
50. *Ethnology of Bengal*, p. 155.
51. *Ibid.*, p. 27.
52. *Ibid.*, p. 30.
53. Hutton, *Angami Nagas*, 28 *sq.*, 364.
54. Keith, *Antiquity of Man*, p. 159.
55. Tylor, *Early History of Mankind*, p. 228 *sq.*
56. Man, *The Andaman Islanders*, p. 82. Census Report, 1901, p. 50.
57. Crooke, *Popular Religion and Folklore of Northern India*, ii. 193.
58. *Ethnographic Notes in Southern India*, p. 466.
59. *Ibid.*, p. 469.
60. *Castes and Tribes of S. India*, vol. iii. 11.

61. *Ibid.*, vol. ii. 385.
62. *Ibid.*, vol. i. 99.
63. *Ibid.*, vol. i. 119.
64. *The Lushei Kuki Clans*, p. 103 and p. 86.
65. *The Sema Nagas*, p. 180.
66. Anthropological Essays presented to E. B. Tylor, p. 23.
67. *Early History of Mankind*, p. 246. (1878 Edn.)
68. Anthropological Essays presented to E. B. Tylor, p. 23.
69. *Ibid.*, p. 40.
70. Bureau of American Ethnology, *Bulletin* 60, part 1, p. 155. *Cf. Journal Royal Anthropological Institute*, vol. 36, p. 13.
71. Man, *Andaman Islanders*, p. 159.
72. *Ibid.*, p. 161.
73. ERE, xi. 875 d. *The Angami Nagas*, p. 403 *sq.*
74. *The Angami Nagas*, p. 79, p. 405.
75. *Burmese Sketches*, ii. 356. *The Khasis*, p. 12. *The Angamis*, p. 404.
75a. *The American Indian* (Clark Wissler), p. 122, p. 243.
76. *Descriptive Ethnology of Bengal*, p. 153.
77. *Linguistic Survey of India*, vol. iv., p. 247.
78. *Tribes and Castes of Central Provinces*, iv. p. 123.
79. *The Khasis*, p. 58.
80. *The Angamis*, p. 63.
81. *The Andaman Islanders*, p. 154.
82. *The Naga Tribes of Manipur*, p. 48.
83. *The Angamis*, p. 64.
84. *The Lushei Kuki Clans*, p. 29.
85. *The Semas*, p. 53.
86. Census Report, 1901, vol. iii., p. 66.
87. *Descriptive Ethnology of Bengal* p. 20 Report on the Condition of the Santals. p. 67.

LECTURE III.

The Linguistics of the Lower Culture—Variability and Imitations—The Classificatory System of Relationship—Principles of Loans—General Characteristics, Concreteness, Lack of Abstracts—Effect of General Conditions—Phonetics and Tones—Education in the Lower Culture—Special Linguistics—Secret and Special Languages—Sign and Gesture—Language—Tabus on Names as Things—Legends and Myths—Folklore and Poetry—Dances.

What can we learn of the mental habits of the lower culture by studying the language spoken there? Shall we learn what will interest us most from the structure of the languages, or from the vocabularies, or from the way in which new ideas or things are dealt with and spoken of? There is a deal of social history and social effort in every word, since there must at least be a concord between speaker and hearer as to the significance and import of the sounds. Yet as M. Levy Bruhl fitly reminds us, " Il est probable que par suite des migrations des melanges des absorptions de groupes les uns par les autres, nous ne rencontrons nulle part une langue correspondant exactement a la mentalitè qui s'exprime dans ses représentations collectives " (1). The classical instance of " the rapidity with which a community may change all the characteristics which are generally supposed to indicate its race " (2) is to be found in the tangle of tribes on the North-East Frontier of India, all in a relatively low state of culture, where " in two generations all but the vaguest traces of their origin are lost " (3). Languages are changed with every few miles of migration. Indeed, it is characteristic of these languages that they soon split up into dialects which are not mutually intelligible. Thus as Hutton tells the tale. Among the Semas " Seven men of different villages happened to meet by the road one evening. They asked one another what they had got with them to eat with their rice. Each mentioned a different thing, *atusheh*, *gwomishi*, *mugishi*, *amusa*, *akelhe*, etc., including as some understood it, dried fish, meat, and various kinds of vegetables. They agreed to pool their good things and share alike, and sat down prepared for a feast, each one thinking how he had scored by agreeing to share with his neighbours. When they opened their loads, they all produced chillies " (**3**). In the nature of these forms of speech are tendencies to variation and elements making for the formation of dialectical differences, just as there are groups marked by " a peculiar vagabond strain " (**4**).

When describing the classificatory system as " one of the great landmarks in the history of mankind," Sir James Frazer finely puts it that " the distinction between the system of group relationship and the system of individual relationship coincides, broadly speaking, with the distinction between savagery and civilisation; the boundary between the lower and the higher strata of humanity runs approximately on the line between the two different modes of counting kin, the one mode counting it by groups the other by individuals. Reduced to its most general terms, the line of cleavage is between collectivism and individualism; savagery stands on the side of collectivism; civilisation stands on the side of individualism " (**5**). I myself have found that what affects one member of a social group is believed to affect others of his social group, so that " The sense of social solidarity is such that all members of the social unit are constrained by custom to regard the tabued object as potentially dangerous by them, and therefore to be avoided " (**6**). Thus in studying the cases, as we find them in India, where the classificatory system—either in full vigour or in a modified but still identifiable form, continues to indicate the structure of social units and their relations, we may note this expression of social mentality as conclusive evidence of the social interests of the groups examined.

It has long been known that " The Dravidians are in possession of a complete and typical system of the classificatory or group system of relationship" (**7**). Much has to be done ere we can determine the part which the South of India has played in the long past in shaping the social scheme as it now exists for " many of the greatest Hindu teachers were Dravidians and at the present day it is in the Dravidian region that the temples are most splendid, the Brahmans strictest and most respected "(**8**). Among the Birhors, that broken wandering folk of the hills and jungles of Chota Nagpur, Sarat Chandra Roy finds the classificatory system in force, with special features due to clan exogamy and the recognition of kinship through the father's side (**9**). The evidence of " language " is striking and unmistakeable. " The Birhor uses the same kinship term (*Mamu*) for his mother's brother and his father's sister's husband, and similarly the same term (*Hatom*) is used for the father's sister and the mother's brother's wife and to this day cross-cousin marriage in which these two relationships are combined in one and the same person, is not unknown in this tribe " (**10**). From the most backward of the tribes speaking Munda languages I turn to the Khasis, the most advanced, at any rate in linguistic power, of this group and there find a prohibition against the marriage with a daughter of a man's mother's brother so long as that uncle is alive (**11**). By reason of this notable prohibition, due, as I think, to the development of Khasi society on special lines (**12**) there is no common term for maternal uncle and father-in-law as in the cases such as Garo, where these marriages are prescribed or preferred. But as evidence of the order of things which once existed, this relation, *'U Kni*, as he is called, is also the husband of the father's sister, thus preserving an archaic feature of social structure. In the term *Kha* for male relations, we have direct evidence of the recognition of male kinship side by side with a matrilineal system developing from conditions still prevailing among the Garos. Among the Sema Nagas, " If otherwise suitable, marriage with the mother's brother's daughter, or father's sister's son, is preferred " **(14)**. This preference finds expression in the use of one and the same term *Angu*, for mother's brother and wife's father and of the same term *Ani* (which is a common Naga and Kuki form) for the father's sister, and the husband's mother **(15)**. Sema terms of relationship exhibit curious features which may be due to the extraordinary social history of this very mixed people **(16)**. Thus in Dravidian, in Munda and in Tibeto-Burman forms of speech are preserved linguistic forms which can be correlated with modes of social structure, typically associated with lower culture.

Nothing in their experience can be more " concrete " more direct and constant in interest than the behaviour which by social custom they have to observe towards other members of the group in which they live. Thus the classification of persons with whom by marriage and by the rules relating to marriageability they have special relations, is obviously a matter of prime interest, since the " classificatory system," as it is called, of relationship is found in its most notable forms among people whose languages afford evidence of a very low power of classification in general. Only the special prominence given in social attention to the matters which are associated by custom with the various relations, can explain this feature of their mental life, and it behoves us to search diligently for the principles on which the classificatory system is based, a task to which I shall return later when discussing social structure.

On what principle does one language borrow words from another? We read that " Whereas other Nagas readily borrow new words from Assamese or Hindustani and assimilate them into their own tongue (this is particularly noticeable in Sema) the Angami invents a word of purely Angami form. Thus an Angami speaks of a steamboat as *mi-ru,* literally fire-boat, while the Sema who on the Angami principle could perfectly well coin the word *ami-shuka,* would never dream of using anything but *jahaz,* even when speaking in his own tongue to other Semas. Similarly, while the Angami always speaks of a gun as *Misi* (= fire-stick) the ordinary word used by the Sema is *alika,* which really means the cross-bow used by his Chang and Sangtam neighbours, or *mashcho,* which seems to be borrowed from the Angami word" (**17**). In a note we find that "Some Angamis who went with the Naga Labour Corps to France saw aeroplanes for the first time, but were at no loss at all for a word, dubbing them *kepronya* (= flying machines) without hesitation" (**18**). Is there anything to show why one group should borrow freely from foreign sources while its neighbour should ingeniously invent words true to the current form ? Am I wrong in saying that we have cases of word formation on natural principles in instances such as the Kukis who give the name *Miaocha* to the harmless necessary cat ? There are Munda speaking folk who call it *Pusi* (**19**). There are descriptive words such as *cheklaobi,* the Meithei for a snipe which means the bird that calls *chek chek.* There are words which enshrine a local myth as the Meithei *Nong-Thāng-Kuppa,* the flash of the Rain God's dao.

I remember my interest in this aspect of mental activity when a Thado Kuki, who was quite unacquainted with tents, without hesitation described my tent as "*pōn-in*" literally cloth-house, as do the Angamis, Lhotas, Semas and Changs (letter from Mr. Hutton). As a matter of curiosity upon comparing the various words for gun in the hill dialects, I find that the Meithei calls it *Nongmei,* meaning thunder-fire, the Lushei calls it *Si-lai,* the Lakher call it *Mei-Thei-Paw,* the Thado call it *Mepum,* while in Kachin a flint lock is *Miba.* The word for fire, *mei,* appears in these words, including the Kachin form, though the actual word for fire in Kachin seems to be *wān,* which seems to be related to the form *bān,* commonly meaning sky in many dialects. Whatever the exact meaning of the Lushei word, *silai,* it is clearly a local word. In Chang it is *nemthing*—iron tube. Konyak and Ao have words of the same import. In Ao it is *prang-pung,* said to mean the prang tube. an onomato-poeic compound. We may therefore conclude that all these people drew on the resources of their own language for a word for gun, using various methods, analogy, visual and auditory description, concrete description, etc. Yet the thing itself came to them from external sources. To turn to another area and another linguistic family, I find that the word for iron in Santali and Mundari *Mārhāt* (**20**) conforms to local structure, but in the broken speech of folk such as the Birhors, the Juangs and Kharrias (**21**) who all get their supplies of the metal from Bengali traders, it is *loha,* an Indo-Aryan iron word. The Santals and Mundas are people who have developed a strong economic system, and are able to maintain themselves and their institutions against external pressure more successfully than feeble folk like the Birhors. The village smith is a member in many cases of the group, not an outsider. It is quite legitimate to infer that many groups in the lower culture are able of their own material in their own speech, to invent new words to describe new objects. But before we can formulate any definite principle for the preference in any given case of a loan word over a word of indigenous fabrication the general circumstances of the intercourse between the groups have to be known, and it is possible that as in the case of other novelties weight must be allowed to the prestige factor.

As to the general characters of languages of the lower culture in India, Sir George Grierson says of the Munda languages that " they belong to that class which possesses a richly varied stock of words to denote individual things and ideas, but is extremely poor in general and abstract terms. . . . In a similar way nouns denoting relationship are seldom conceived in the abstract, but a pronominal suffix restricting the sphere of the idea is usually added " (**22**). The languages of the hills of Assam (except Khasi, which is a member of the Austric family and has evolved on distinct lines, arriving at a grammatical device by means of which at will any root can be treated as an abstract) exhibit the same characters, the richly varied stock of words, the absence of abstract terms, the rigid definition of relationship terms by pronominal prefixes (**23**). Precisely the same phenomenon is found in other parts of the world as in America and in Melanesia where, as Dr. Rivers tells us (**24**) " The nouns which take the true possessive pronoun in Melanesia are of three kinds ; terms of relationship ; terms for parts of the body, and terms denoting expecially close possession." To the trend towards individual ownership and individual relations which were started by the contact of the indigenous inhabitants with immigrants who disturbed the communal organisation of the country they invaded, are ascribed these features of Melanesian linguistics. In the same way the importance of the body, due to foreign ideas, gave " to parts of the body that social interest which made a definite system of nomenclature necessary." Be it remembered in this connection that terms of relationship are classificatory, so that " The term ' father ' for instance, is applied to all those whom the father would call brother, and to all the husbands of those whom the mother calls ' sister,' both brother and sister being used in a far wider sense than among ourselves " (**25**). The trend towards individualisation which is civilisation is variously marked. As to individual ownership of property, while there are evidences of communal rights in certain forms of property, as where thatching grass

" is usually village or clan property " (**26**), it may be said to be well established, since it extends to " special trees though they may grow on the land of another person—so much so that a dispute will arise as to the ownership of a tree which is actually growing on the ground of a third person not a party to the dispute " (**27**). The use of possessive affixes to parts of the body which, after all, survives in our own speech since we say, " I have washed my hands," when a Frenchman says, " I have washed the hands," may be susceptible of the simple explanation that the most elementary advance in consciousness is that of self as distinct from other members of the same group, so that the use of possessives would follow on this fact. Languages such as Santali have preserved forms of inclusive and exclusive plurals, which might, as in Melanesia, " have arisen through a definite social need, a need for the distinction between acts performed by one or both of two peoples living in close intercourse with one another and yet preserving in large measure their own customs and interests " (**28**). The features of Santali society, composed of clans—each marked from the others by separate " passwords," and separate group worship, with strong social solidarity—may be deemed to afford the elements required for the social need called in to explain this phenomenon in Melanesia.

At the same time Naga society is composed of clans, each acting as independent social units in many matters of social interest, but there seem to be no precise indications of the use of the linguistic device of inclusive and exclusive plurals among Naga tribes. It may be that the device exists but has not been recorded. It may be that it does not exist because the Naga tribes on their travels from their original home have absorbed other groups on terms of equality. Intermarriages, the practice of local rather than clan exogamy and the development of sub-groups (**29**) may also explain the absence of this feature.

What, then, are we to make of the habit of mind disclosed by the possession of a "richly varied vocabulary" in which "the different varieties of some particular animal are denoted by means of different terms where we should use one and the same word"? Can we be satisfied with the explanation that it is the outcome of "a tendency to coin a separate word for every individual concrete conception"? As Sir George Grierson reminds us in the passage from which I have quoted, "This peculiarity is shared by most languages spoken by tribes in a primitive stage of civilisation **(30)**. This tendency to concreteness of expression is associated intelligibly enough with a poverty of abstract ideas, or rather of linguistic devices to express abstract ideas which may be a different thing. In estimating the nature and extent of this tendency to concreteness of expression, be it remembered that evidence of the power of these groups of the lower culture to classify and systematise their conditions in linguistic expression is afforded by the existence among them of the classificatory system in whole or in part. Be it also remembered that as we have seen they extend their field of experience by allowing equal even superior validity to dreams and other impressions derived from the uncontrolled activities of the lower levels of consciousness which they interpret either conventionally or by reference to special persons which has much the same practical effect as the conventional method. It is clear that every individual specimen of any one of the varieties of some particular animal (which varieties are denoted by means of different terms), will be described by the same term as any other individual member of the same variety, and be identified with all the other individual members of that variety. "In Lushei we find nine words for 'ant' and twenty different translations of the one word 'basket.'" There are doubtless nine kinds of ant which an expert entomologist would classify correctly, but they are different kinds. There are many uses to which a basket may be put and the shape and size of basket suitable for one purpose are not suitable for other purposes. They are different things, and are spoken of and recognised as different things. The "interest" differs in each case, in kind as in degree. After all, systematists in modern science do not appear to be in perfect accord at all times in all matters pertaining to their craft, so that the evidence of the nature and extent in the lower culture of classification in matters of special interest has peculiar value to us in forming a correct estimate of their conditions.

The test is a fair one, since the language of a group is significant in a high degree of the mental life of that group. By this test, then, the lower culture is characterised by definite features in its linguistics, and in framing further estimates of their activities in other directions the evidence of linguistics as to the concreteness of their mental attitudes must be taken into account.

We know something in this country of the idea that "Le progrés de la civilisation s'est produit par une action reciproque de la main sur l'esprit et de l'esprit sur la main" (**31**). It is characteristic of this level of culture where there is no machinery that everything tends to be individual, distinct. May I quote myself once again? A chance remark may let in more light than all the careful inquiries and systematic notes. I was once in a village far from the beaten track and had shown them the magic lantern. I had given them practical illustrations of the utility of a repeating pistol; I had amused them with a galvanic battery, and when all was over, I was enjoying their hospitality by the camp fire and had listened to tales of the bad old days when they were left severely alone by restraining influences. The conversation flagged until I asked a man who had hung about me all day what of all that I had shown was the most surprising to him. That started a discussion which ended in a verdict that the strangest thing that the Sahib-log had brought within their ken was coined money, and on further inquiry I found that its uniformity was the special feature which had so excited their interest. Nor is this to be wondered at, for at the level of their civilisation all their crafts are innocent of machinery; everything they make tends to variety, everything is individual. This feature of their material life is reflected in their language, for they have a separate name for articles and actions which we classify together. They insist on the points of difference while we classify by identities" (**32**).

A chance incident may reveal a social ideal. I was busy learning Thado Kuki and had reached the stage where "useful phrases," conversational small talk were being acquired. I asked of my interpreter what is the Thado for I have enough to eat. *Ka-va-tai*. Now what is the Thado for I have enough to drink—*Zu ka-kam-tai*. Proud in the possession of polite useful phrases, I went on, and reached my next village ahead of my coolies and interpreter. As in duty bound, they brought out stoops of *zu*, for the rice beer is refreshing to a weary man, and when I had had a glass I tried the new phrase. *Zu ka-kam-tai*, I said, gracefully waving away the dusky Hebe. The village immediately dissolved into laughter, and I feared I had said something improper when I merely meant to be grateful. When the interpreter arrived I asked him what "*zu ka-kam-tai*" meant. Huzur, he said, it means to be dead drunk. Then I saw that the limit of saturation for a Kuki was not mine, in the matter of rice beer.

A word as to what may be learnt from a study of the phonetics and of the grammar of languages of the lower culture. There are preserved by groups of the lower culture methods of using sound which have either been discarded or have never been possessed by more advanced groups. There are phonetic differences which, as Dr. Rivers surmised of those characterising Melanesian languages, "must be due to definite structural differences in the organs of speech, and it is most unlikely that these could be produced by such differences of environment as exist within the regions" (**33**). Thus far-reaching identifications may be effected by the scientific investigation and correlation of phonetic data, especially those recorded among groups of the lower culture, since, as Mr. Richards has urged, "the typical Jungle Tribe of South India does not speak a typical Dravidian tongue, but a grotesque caricature of it" (**34**).

As to the more prominent features of social mentality as they seem to be revealed by the set forms or grammatical structure of languages of the lower culture, I do not think we shall ever reach a true estimate of the real significance of the social effort involved in the establishment of so many different organised modes of communicating with fellow men, members of the same social group, as to common needs, until we depart fully from our own traditionalism. It ought to be possible, as Sir Richard Temple urged years ago, to frame a theory of Universal grammar (**35**). Various are the devices which are used in the lower culture for grammatical purposes. Complexity marks the methods of the Andamanese dialects where they use prefixes whose function is purely to modify the meaning of a root, and so to form, in combination with the root, a pure stem, (**36**) prefixes to indicate personal possession of an intimate nature, where there is classification (an important piece of evidence of their mental power) of things animate and inanimate. Or take the Santali verb whose mysteries are sketched in outline by Sir George Grierson (**37**) and consider the ingenuity of a language which can convert any word into a verb by adding a simple suffix. Or again, in the Tibeto-Burman dialects there are languages with a wealth of tones (**38**), others that employ determinatives to bring out shades of meaning with a remarkable precision (**39**), others, again, using couplets, grammatical complexity and grammatical order, but all efficient in their purposes. But all this comes slowly; these phenomena are the work of many generations. There have been changes, for in the songs and popular ritual formulas are preserved archaic modes of speech often now so mutilated as to have become completely unintelligible. Rich is the harvest which awaits the scholar who shall take in hand the comparative analysis of the archaic speech as preserved in the song and ritual of the lower culture and trace the life history of the speech, for there is a "biology of speech," and laws of that science can be best discovered by examination of the lower culture and its forms of speech, for which there is available much material from India. Nor are we concerned only with the diversity and range of linguistic devices as evidence of the power of the human mind. They afford evidence of the strength and constancy of social life. Thus special importance attaches to the institutions created in and by society by means of which the education of the lower culture is carried on and the traditions preserved without the artificial aid of writing. The elements are often obvious enough which make for variation and modification of the mental life of the lower culture, but at the same time the elements and factors in social life which make for continuity and stability possess a vitality and vigour altogether remarkable.

EDUCATION.

The educational system of the lower culture is simple. It centres in an Institution known as the Men's House, which, as Hutton Webster has shown, is of world-wide occurrence **(40)**. In India we know it as the Morung or Kichuki of the Nagas **(41)**; the Pākhonvāl of the Meitheis **(42)**; the Nokpante of the Garos **(43)**; the Zawl-buk of the Lushais **(44)**; the Mandaghar of the Bhuiyas **(45)**; the Giti-ora of the Mundas and Birhors **(46)**; the Jonkh-erpa of the Oraons, Malers, Maria Gonds, Kandhs **(47)**, the Gotalgarh of the Gonds of

Chattisgarh and the Feudatory States (**48**), while the Kurumbas know it as " the pundugar chavadi, meaning literally the abode of vagabonds " (**49**). It is not universal since the Santals have it not. They have, however, a village official, the Jagmanjhi, " whose most important duty is apparently to look after the morals of the boys and girls, and if he is at all straightlaced, they must often lead him a hard life of it . . . and Jagmanjhis have admitted to me that they have plenty of such love affairs to arrange " (**50**). The Khasis do not have this, but they are acquainted with it among their neighbours, the Bhois and Lalungs, for they have a special word, *ka trang* (**51**) for it. The Andamanese Jarawas, the widest group, build in the rains a communal hut, which shelters several families (**52**), and custom demands that " even at the homes they are careful to maintain this order, viz., of placing the bachelors and spinsters at either end of the building and the married couples in the space between " (**53**). Among the Meitheis the house itself is no longer built, but the words, Pākhonvāl and Ningonvāl, show that they once possessed this institution, and they still have village officers, the Pākhonlakpa and Ningonlakpa, who correspond to the Jagmanjhi of the Santals (**54**). It is disappearing among Nagas, for we find that with the Semas " It is occasionally found in a miniature form not unlike a model of a Lhota morung. Such a model is often built in times of scarcity, the underlying idea apparently being that the scarcity may be due to the village having neglected to conform to a custom which has been abandoned. . . . A miniature morung of this sort is always built when a new village is made (**55**).

" In these days when alarms and excursions are no longer in the order of things, it is only used " on the occasions of ceremonies and gennas which, by traditional usage, call for a house definitely allotted to the young men of the clan. . . . At other times it is used merely as a casual resort for the village bucks and perhaps as an occasional sleeping place . . . among the Memi they are used by the young girls as well as the young men both in some cases using the same house, the young men sleeping on an upper shelf and the girls below them. The publicity probably entails great propriety of behaviour" (**56**). It was a guard house. It was the sleeping place of the men of the community except the very old, who alone were allowed to sleep in the village. The Old Kukis (Chiru, Kom and Tikhup) allowed no woman to enter these buildings (**56a**). Its social importance lies in the fact that it was "a useful seminary for training young men in their social and other duties and an institution for magico-religious observances calculated to secure success in hunting and to augment the procreative power of the young men" (**57**). The Pax Britannica, the spread of Christian morality, economic progress have contributed to the decay of the institution which had its abuses as well as its uses (**58**). There are grades, age-grades, in the adolescent life. Thus among the Oraons a boy is admitted at about **11** or **12** years of age, when he is called a Puna Jokhar. Three years later he becomes a Majh-turia Jokhar or lad of the middle grade, in which he stays for three years at the end of which he becomes a Koha Jokhar, retaining his membership of the Institution to all intent and purposes till he has one or two children (**59**).

The interesting feature is that the education in social matters is largely carried on by the adolescents themselves, orally and by example, on purely traditional lines.

The formation of special groups, isolated by social reasons, within a society, leads to specialisation in the use of words of the common stock and as Meillet (**60**) has shown, the opposite is true, viz., that a word may pass from a special group to the common stock. The lack of economic specialisation in the lower structure is characteristic. But equally characteristic are the clearly marked divisions by age and sex, by social standing, by relationship, so that there are features in the social life of the lower culture which, given the necessary conditions, would facilitate special linguistic developments by specialisation consequent on parallel, conterminous or aterminous associations. Thus as a result of the special functions which women perform in the social economy, there have developed in many groups special words used only by women, whose influence as a factor producing variation would be enhanced by the possibility of local exogamy, bringing in women of alien stock, as mothers, directing the early education of the young.

There are secret languages as with the Todas **(61)**, who are often brought into intercourse with Badagas and Tamils, from whom they seek by this means to keep their conversation secret. Mr. Hutton finds that " There is a practice which seems to be known in most Sema villages of inverting or altering the order of words in a sentence or of syllables in a word, so as to make the language meaningless gibberish to anyone not knowing the slang. There does not seem to be any fixed system on which this is done. . . . There does not seem to be any very real advantage gained by the use of this slang beyond that of being able to irritate one's neighbours who do not know it, by speaking it in their presence. . . . At the same time it is said that the Sema slang is used with some effect in trade, as it is possible for one man to warn another that the price asked by a third is too high. . . . This slang is also said to be useful in intrigues and undoubtedly is used to make offensively personal remarks and to abuse strangers who do not understand it. . . . In one Sema village, apparently the only one, Aichisagami, the whole village has acquired this slang, and to such an extent that it has almost become the ordinary language of the village and is normally used by the people of the village in speaking to one another. . . . The result of this in Aichisagami has been the production of secondary slangs based on the first, which are spoken by a number of the villagers in the same way that what may be called primary slang is used in other villages (**62**)." This is perhaps an exceptional case, but it gives an indication of a way in which the diversity of dialects characterising this area may have arisen, and the alterations may, it is clear, extend to the order of the words, thus modifying the structure as a whole.

Can we say that the languages of the lower culture as I have sketched them, are on an artificial not a natural basis of thought ? Is there any relation between the spoken language and what is called the language of signs ? Pieces of charred wood, chillies, bullets, stones, splintered bamboos, all these things are used as messages (**63**), whose import, whose meanings as symbols, are clear to all. Perhaps with development of graphic art, this method of communication may become more extended. But it is to the use of sign or manual language that I must turn. Parler avec les mains, c'est á la lettre, dans une certaine mesure, penser avec les mains. . . . Si donc la langue orale décrit et dessine, dans le dernier detail, les positions, les mouvements, les distances, les formes et les contours, c'est que le langage par gestes emploie précisement ces moyens d'expression (**64**). " Among the Angami Nagas the language of signs has reached a high state of development . . . indeed the writer has known a dumb man make a long and detailed complaint of an assault in which nothing was missing except proper names, and even these were eventually identified by means of the dumb man's description of his assailants dress and personal appearance " (**65**).

This visual language is not symbolic, not as the message system referred to above, but is descriptive and concrete. Herein we may ponder the findings of the French linguist who holds that " Le langage visuel est probablement aussi ancien que le langue auditif . . . la plus part des langages visuels en usage aujourd'hui sont simplement dérivés du langage auditif " (**65a**).

Words are possessed of a concreteness, a value, a significance in social life such that it is sometimes customary to place a ban upon words which by their association with sacred things or persons are thought to be able to influence the affairs of man. Thus a tabu is placed by the Mal Saren Santals on the word *mal* " when engaged in a religious ceremony or when sitting on a panchayat to determine tribal questions " (**66**) at the moments when their membership of the group is in special prominence. A Savara has no name for a numeral above twelve because " One day, long ago, some Saoras were measuring grain in a field, and when they had measured 12 measures of some kind, a tiger pounced in on them and devoured them " (**67**). I know of a village whose chief, a religious rather than a secular authority, if such a distinction be in any degree valid, " must not use abusive language to anyone whatever the provocation, nor must he lay an imprecation on anyone " (**68**) because so sacred is he as *the* man of the village that his word would have power to destroy since his words and acts are needed to make the village prosper.

Among the Angamis, " Bad language must be avoided while a child's first cloth is being woven, as if bad language is used under such circumstances the child that wears it will be affected for the worse " (**69**). Variations in the factors which regulate the formation of social values would thus find expression in variations of linguistic values.

LEGENDS AND MYTHS:

I have described the languages of the lower culture in India as preserved without the " artificial aid of writing." There is, however, current among the hill tribes of Assam (**70**) a myth that they once possessed this art but lost it because they used skins while their more prudent neighbours used boards. One day the dogs got at the skins, ate them all, and so destroyed forever the art. One tribe points to a bodkin now used to pin their hair up as the pen they once owned and also as part of the same myth tell how, "to distinguish the sexes apart, the men tied their hair in front while the women tied it behind. . . . The men shortened their cloth and made it into a waistcloth, while the women lengthened their cloth, making of it a petticoat." Arts as useful as that of writing have been lost (71). It is often possible that there may be some shred of truth in these narratives which are told as true, as giving an account of a noted and notable, if negative, feature in their social environment, and are therefore classifiable as myths. What made them think it necessary for them to account for their ignorance of writing ? What made them accept this account of their loss of the art ? As I said of another tale, "We may infer that the particular mechanism of the explanation was selected and the explanation itself accepted because they were in harmony with popular ideas of causation as regards social phenomena of this order. It gives us a glimpse into the minds both of those who invented the tale and of those who accepted it and adopted it as article of faith (72). There clearly has been contact with a society which practises the art of writing, such as the Meithei culture, but as evidence of the mentality which accepts as valid such a tale, it is specially interesting. Risley records Santal myths "concerning the origin of the five additional septs. . . . The eighth tribe, Baske, at first, belonged to the seven, but by reason of their offering their breakfast (*baske*) to the gods while the Santals were still in Champa they were formed into a separate sept under the name of Baske. The Besras (No. 9) were separated on account of the immoral behaviour of their eponym, who was called Besra, the licentious one. The tenth sept, Pauria, are called after the pigeon and the eleventh, Chore, after the lizard ; and the story is that on the occasion of a famous tribal hunting party the members of these two tribes failed to kill anything but pigeons and lizards, so they were called after the names of these animals. The twelfth sept, the Bedea, was left behind and lost when the Santals went up out of Champa. They had no father, so the story goes—at least the mother of their first ancestor could not say who the father was and for this reason they were deemed of lower rank than the other septs." **(73)** These tales are good evidence that Santals consider themselves able to accept some irregular mode of worship, specially licentious behaviour, signally poor luck in hunting on a conspicuous occasion, or illegitimacy, as grounds for the formation of a new group. It is psychological evidence as regards the people who regard these accounts of social divisions as adequately explained by the tale. It is not historical evidence that the divisions were created under the circumstances stated. Of tales whose purpose would seem to be purely aesthetic, there is a store collected from all over India. They may be classified as Contes, " those which seem to be told, not for the explanation of any custom or the handing down of any record, but simply and solely for the sake of the tale itself. Here are fairy tales, animal stories, and cynical observations of human foibles " **(74)**. As psychological documents they possess a significance apart from any evidence yielded by them incidentally for " When a social condition is mentioned incidentally, or is revealed by the general colouring of a myth we can be confident that it is not the pure product of imagination, but has a definite historical value " **(75)**.

In the folk tales told by the people as amusement, for their aesthetic value, resides a mass of interesting information, and one of the puzzles of scientific anthropology is to account for the distribution in many parts of the world of identical tales. Have they travelled during the long ages from one common centre or are they the products of the human mind working on similar experiences, attaining similar results? Convergence, contact, common conditions, independent inventions—to which of these shall we incline ? It is easy in a way to construct hypotheses as to the transmission, through a series of intermediaries, of a tale found to be common to both Naga and Santal, such as the Naga tale of the Rat Princess and the Greedy Man (**76**). Actual direct transmission would be impossible by reason of the fundamental differences of language.

Of the poetry of the lower culture there are in the songs of the Nagas as recorded and translated by Mr. Hutton, sure evidence of a real poetical sense, " Behind their spontaneous geniality lies a vein of deep melancholy. The thought of death is never far from them, and the fear of it is a potent factor in their lives. . . . There is a tendency in the vast majority of their songs to animadvert on the brevity of life and the dread finality of death." As an example at random it may not be out of place to give a rough rendering of a part-song sung at the Thekrangi genna by the young men and girls of Khonoma and being in point of fact of an almost flirtatious tendency.

MEN. Seeds are in the earth and seeds keep falling to the earth.
Men take them away but still they spring up,
But if man die, he riseth not again.
WOMEN. Girls, delay not too long to marry.
When your hair groweth long you grow old,
When you grow old you die.
BOTH. The moon waneth yet it waxeth again,
But when I lose my beloved there is no more meeting. (**77**).

DANCES.

In the combination of song and dance, of the spoken expressions of the fancy, the social emotions, and the acted representations of the deeds told of in speech, we have a height of aesthetic attainment to which the lower culture often attains. Sir W. Ridgeway avers that " wide induction leads irresistibly to the conclusion that Tragedy and serious Drama, wherever they are found under the sun, have their roots in the world-wide belief in the continued existence of the soul after the death of the body " (**78**).

Throughout the lower culture are found ritual dances always part of cultural complexes now in connection with the honoured dead, now with the agricultural rites which secure prosperity for the living, both of a practical purpose since society, constituted of those that return and in constant relation with those that are separated from them, derives its substance and its wellbeing from this dual estate. "Among the Garos dancing . . . appears to form a very prominent feature of every social function as well as of religious ceremony" **(78a)**. With the Angami Naga "Dancing, singing and dhan-pounding, as a rule, go hand in hand with ceremonial dress . . . the songs sung include both particular songs traditionally associated with the occasion and sometimes in archaic language not fully understood except by those skilled in them as well as songs in common use which may be fancied by the singers" **(79)**.

For the Khasis "dancing forms part of all the Khasi festivities, and is an important adjunct of some of their religious festivities" **(80)**.

The Nongkrem dance, one of the greatest festivals in the Khasi Hills "is really part of what is known as the *pom-blang*, or goat killing ceremony, performed by the Siem of Nongkrem or Khyrim . . . to Ka Blei Synshar the ruling goddess) that the crops may prosper and that there may be a successful era for the people of the State. . . . . A goat is then sacrificed and the sacrifice is followed by a dance of twenty-two men armed with swords and shields and chowries (flyflaps). Having danced before the altar the party returns to the house of the Siem priestess and executes another dance in the great courtyard. The Siem and certain selected persons dance in front of the rishot blei or holy post of Khasi oak inside the house of the Siem priestess, the dancers being entertained with dried fish and ginger. Then follows the great dance of girls and men in front of her house . . . it is only the unmarried girls who dance . . . then there is *ka shad mas tieh*, or the dance of the men. . . . After gyrating for some time two men at a time rapidly approach one another and clash their swords together in mock combat. . . . Dancing forms part of the ceremony of placing the ashes in the sepulchre of the clan " (**81**).

From the Central Provinces and Chota Nagpur comes the same combination of song and dance and imitative action. Mr. Russell observes that "The dances of the Kol tribe consist partly of symbolical enactments of events which they desired to be successfully accomplished. Some variations of the dance, Colonel Dalton states, represent the different seasons and the necessary acts of cultivation that each brings with it. . . . The Bhils danced at their festivals and before battles. . . . The object was to obtain success in battle by going through an imitation of a successful battle beforehand. . . . . The Sola dance of Gonds and Baigas in which they perform the figure of the grand chain of the lancers, only that they strike their sticks together instead of clasping hands as they pass, was probably once an imitation of a combat. It is still sometimes danced before their communal hunting and fishing parties. In these mimetic rehearsals of events with the object of causing them to occur we may perhaps discern the origin of the arts both of acting and dancing. Another, and perhaps later form was the reproduction of important events or those which had influenced history. For to the primitive mind, as already seen, the results were not conceived of as instrumentally caused by the event itself and of its life and personality. Hence by the re-enactment of the event the beneficial results would be again obtained or at least preserved in undiminished potency and vigour. This was perhaps the root idea of the drama and the representation of sacred or heroic episodes on the stage " (**82**).

I carry this further and assert that they dance these dances not as representatives, but as the living reincarnated personalities of those who fought and won these battles who thus made the crops to flourish who in this manner and by these preparations became mighty in the chase, whose distinction and eminence in the arts which are so important to society, were thus achieved and signalised.

1. *Les fonctions mentales dans des Sociétés Inférieures*, p. 151.
2. Census Report, 1911, ix. 184, 186, 193, 249.
3. *The Semas*, p. 266.
4. *The Lushei Kuki Clans*, p. 21.
5. *Folklore of the Old Testament*, ii. 227.
6. *The Naga Tribes of Manipur*, 199 *a*.
7. Frazer, *Totemism and Exogamy*, ii. 241.
8. Eliot, *Hinduism and Buddhism*, I. xxxiii.
9. *Journal of the Bihar and Orissa Research Society*, December, 1917, p. 543.
10. *Ibid.*, p. 548.
11. *The Khasis*, p. 78.
12. *Man In India*, i. (2) 25 *sq*.
13. *Ibid.*, p. 28.
14. *The Semas*, p. 132, p. 141.
15. *Cf.* Dictionaries, Tangkhul, Lushei, Thado, S.V. *Ni*.
16. *The Semas*, p. 379.
17. *The Angamis*, p. 295.
18. *Ibid.*, note.
19. L.S.R., iv. p. 248.
20. *Ibid*, p. 247.
21. *Ibid*, p, 247.
22. L.S.R. iv., p. 23.
23. L.S.R., iii., part 1, p. 5.
24. *History of Melanesian Society*, ii., p. 490.
25. *Kinship and Social Organisation*, p. 3.
26. *The Angamis*, p. 77, p. 141.
27. *Ibid.*, p. 78.
28. *History of Melanesian Society*, ii., p. 487.
29. *The Angamis*, p. 115.
30. L.S.R., iii. part 1, p. 5.
31. Levy Bruhl, *op. cit.*, p. 179.
32. *The Naga Tribes of Manipur*, p. 123.
33. *History of Melanesian Society*, ii., p. 471 ; *cf. Language* (Jespersen), p. 255.
34. Presidential Address to Mythic Society, p. 19.
35. *Journal of the Royal Asiatic Society*, July, 1899.
36. *Ibid.*, p. 17, p. 28.
37. L.S.R., iv., pp. 45–51.
38. L.S.R., iii., part 1, p. 4.
39. *Ibid.*, p. 6.
40. *Primitive Secret Societies*, pp. 1–19.
41. *The Angamis*, p. 49.
42. *The Meitheis*, p. 61, p. 153.

43. *The Garos*, p. 37.
44. *The Kuki Lushei Clans*, p. 21.
45. *Journal of the Bihar and Orissa Research Society*, June, 1919, p. 239.
46. *The Mundas*, p. 385.
47. *Descriptive Ethnology of Bengal*, p. 247.
48. *Tribes and Castes of the Central Provinces*, iii., p. 131.
49. *Castes and Tribes of S. India*, iv. 162.
50. *Descriptive Ethnology of Bengal*, p. 214 ; see also pp. 217, 218.
51. *Khasi-English Dictionary*, s.v. *Ka trang*.
52. Census Report, 1901, vol. iii., pp. 62, 78.
53. *The Andaman Islanders*, p. 40 *n*.
54. *The Meitheis*, p. 61.
55. *The Sema Nagas*, p. 37.
56. *The Angami Nagas*, p. 49.
56a. *Lushai Kuki Clans*, p. 151.
57. *The Oraons*, pp. 211 *sq*.
58. Hahn, *Einfuhrung in das Gebiet der Kols-mission*, p. 64.
59. Hahn, *ibid.*, *The Oraons*, p. 215.
60. *L'Année Sociologique*, ix., p. 14 *sq*.
60a. *Language* (Jespersen), p. 254 *et seq*.
61. *The Todas*, p. 616.
62. *The Sema Nagas*, p. 296 *sq*.
63. *The Angami Nagas*, p. 292.
64. Levy Bruhl, *Les Sociétés Inférieures*, p. 180.
65. *The Angami Nagas*, p. 291.
65a. *Le Langage* (P. Vendryes), p. 9.
66. *Tribes and Castes of Bengal*, ii. 228.
67. *Castes and Tribes of Southern India*, vi., p. 312.
68. *The Naga Tribes of Manipur*, p. 181.
69. *The Angami Nagas*, p. 219.
70. *The Naga Tribes of Manipur*, p. 30.
71. Rivers, *The Disappearance of Useful Arts*.
72. *The Naga Tribes of Manipur*, p. 199 c.
73. *Tribes and Castes of Bengal*, ii. 227.
74. *The Angami Nagas*, p. 253.
75. Rivers, *Sociological Significance of Myth* ; *Folklore*, xxiii., p. 311.
76. *The Angami Nagas*, p. 272 ; *Folklore of the Santal Parganas*, p. 168.
77. *The Angami Nagas*, p. 39.
78. *Dramas and Dramatic Dances*, p. 385.
78a. *The Garos*, p. 54.
79. *The Angamis*, p. 194.
80. *The Khasis*, p. 155
81. *The Khasis*, pp. 156, 157.
82. *Tribes and Castes of the Central Provinces*, i. 128.

LECTURE IV.

SOCIAL STRUCTURE.

Social Structure—Sex Divisions—Teknonymy—Kinship and Social Grouping—Exogamy and True Dual Organisation—Cross-Cousin Marriages—Break Up of Dual Organisation—Cases of Specific Exogamy —Free Exogamy.

All human societies are composed of individual men and women. All need food. Children are unable to procure food for themselves for a period of some duration without the help of adults who win their food and that of the children dependent on them from the material provided by their physical environment. In time the child becomes adult, physically mature, able to take an active part in the food-quest, able, if a female, to bear children. In course of time that adult dies. Some of these stages in the life of the individual are quite clearly marked by visible physical changes. The fundamental elements of the groupings of human beings, called human societies, rest on the necessity of food and the biological conditions (if the group is to continue) of producing and rearing children. Man is a *zoon politikon* by reason of the relatively long immaturity of the human young. The fashionable and elaborate comparisons with the other orders of Primates are only remotely relevant since the main characteristic of human society as I see it, is the manner in which the mind of man, as moulded by his life with his fellows, interprets, explains, adapts and modifies the data of the physical environment. Man, the rebel, acts on the ideas which he forms of his relations both with his physical environment and with his human environment, which consists primarily of the members of the group to which he belongs, and then secondarily of the members of other human groups. He is never completely free of the restraint which the elementary facts of his physical nature impose on him. His freedom consists in the slow, laborious discipline of submission which teaches that the conquest of nature is by obedience to partnership, by observation to knowledge and intimacy.

MAIN DIVISIONS.

There are social divisions directly based on natural or biological distinctions. As a result of the "ideas" which men form of their relations to natural phenomena, there are social divisions based on the concepts formed in and by society of human maturity, concepts which are but distantly influenced by physical data. Thus social and physical maturity, as evidenced by marriageability, may, and sometimes do, coincide, but in many cases are separated by social convention. M. Van Gennep puts the case thus: Il convient donc de distinguer de la puberté physique la puberté sociale, de même qu'on distingue entre une parenté physique (consanguinité) et une parenté sociale, entre une maturité physique et une maturité sociale (majorité) etc. (1). In some groups, again, the mature are for some purposes divided into those that are married and fertile, and those that are married but infertile. There are also groups whose bond of union is physical relationship and groups where the principle of union is based on social views consequent on mere propinquity, as there are also groups formed by recognition of common interests, common difficulties, common knowledge, common habitation. And the dead form groups in relation to the living.

The main lines, therefore, in our classification are those of (*a*) sex; (*b*) maturity, and (*c*) relationship. Each of these, again, is subdivided by reason of the difference between social and natural demarcations. Add thereto the fertility division as a sub-grouping of social maturity and we have at least seven distinct—or distinguishable—divisions. Some are, of course, permanently distinguished from the others. There are distinctions of dress, coiffure and ornaments. In some cases it is possible to identify the division only by reason of its emergence, as specially qualified for some social purpose, on some occasion of social action. Every one of those divisions is composed of individuals and is therefore constantly changing its component units. The moments when an individual enters into, or departs from, any one of these divisions are moments when the constitution of the division is modified, when the poise of the division is disturbed, when the individuality of the individual stands out in contrast to the solidarity of the division which he disturbs by his entering or departure. Adjustments have to be made both in and by the division which loses a unit and in and by the division which gains a unit. Those adjustments are effected by action on the part of the divisions affected by the movement. The nature, as society sees it, of the necessity for these periodical adjustments and the ideas current in the groups as to the means to be employed to effect these adjustments can be deduced from a study of the rites performed on on these occasions. The degrees of " individuality " are observable, and therefore recognised, utilised in social adjustments (**1a**).

It is said that only Parliament can turn a woman into a man, but in Lushai society there are " men known as Tuai who dressed as women and did women's work " (**2**). There are occupations specially reserved for women. Thus weaving is women's work all through the Assam Hills where, however, some tribes do not allow their womenfolk to make cloths (**3**). Again " Up to this point (the shaping of the pot) the whole process is performed by women, men not being allowed to touch the pots or even to approach too closely during their preparation as this would cause them to break during the firing. The women of the household are genna on the day of pot-making, speaking to no one outside their household, and their own men folk even may not be spoken to by them or come close to them, after once having left the house in the morning, until the raw pots have been placed on the shelf over the fire " (4).

While in many parts of India there are special rites for the prosperity of the crops which can only be performed by women as described by Dr. Crooke (5), among the Oraons " Should a woman happen to drive the plough, even for a minute, the whole village would be thrown into consternation, as drought and famine would be apprehended as the consequence . . . in any case a " Rogkhedna " expedition has to be undertaken by the village. . . . The touch of a woman, it is believed, impairs the strength and effectiveness of a plough and of certain other implements and weapons. If an Oraon cultivator, while driving the plough feels thirsty and asks his wife or daughter to hand over a cup of water to him, he must for the nonce leave hold of his plough to take the cup of water in order that a female may not come in contact with the plough. Similarly a sword or shield is believed to lose its sharpness or effectiveness through the touch of a woman. The rule prohibiting a woman to thatch a house appears to be based on a similar consideration. Should a woman be found getting up on the thatch of a house, disease and death to some inmate or inmates of the house and misfortune to the village in general are apprehended and a *rogkhedna* expedition has to be undertaken." (6) The agricultural implement of the woman is the digging stick. The plough is the novelty. May be, too, a woman would lose her " effectiveness " if she handled dangerous novelties like the plough or the men's peculiar weapon. From the Kols is found that " eigentumliche Sitte der Frauenkrieg " when " die jungen Frauen and Mädchen sich hoch aufschürzen das Oberkleid und fast neckt, mit Stöcken und Äxten bewaffnet, wie Furien durchs Dorf stürmen und die alle

Hühner and Schweine tot-schlagen, die sie finden. Die Männer und Junglings durfen sich auf der Strasse nicht sehen lassen, sonst werden auch sie von der aufgeregten kreischenden und tobenden Frauenbande angegriffen." (**7**) This orgiastic rite is performed when there is a drought or epidemic sickness. The association of woman with agricultural rites, part of the scheme for procuring the necessities of life, is well shown in the gennas of the Tangkhuls who have two rope-pulling festivals when the women and girls pull against the men and boys by the first of which the omens for the year's harvest are determined (**8**). In the Naga area we find the temporary separation of the sexes at moments of grave social import as the Sekrengi genna (**9**) among the Angamis when male children leave the " women's side, eminently a stage in their social career, and when the health of the community for the coming year is assured or the Thewuukukwu genna (**10**) which marks the cutting of the *ahu dhan.* At the Thekrangi genna there is " dancing and singing on the part of the young men, boys and girls who are unmarried, or married, but who have no children "(**11**).

Among the Chirus, Koms and Purum and Old Kukis " The young women also have houses in which they gather at time of festivals " (**12**).

The custom of teknonymy is undoubtedly in some cases a token of the distinction drawn in social order between the fertile and the sterile. It is found among the Lushais, who have given ingenious but unsatisfying explanations of its origin and purpose among them, (**13**), among the Khasis (**14**), the Garos (**15**), the Kachins (**16**), where in decent society the word " wife " is considered " too coarse in speaking of one's own wife, and a man should speak of her as " my child's mother.' "

It must clearly be viewed as part of the general mass of social institutions and customs. " Le changement de nom est l'un des rites du baptême, de l'initiation, du mariage, de l'intronisation c'est donc aussi comme un rite de passage, de categorisation dans un nouveau groupe special, qu'il convient d'interpreter la tecnonymie " (**17**). The full significance and meaning of the name and the changes made in the name of the individual as he progresses through the stages of social life are clearly and directly related to the phases of the " cycle of life."

TABUS ON WOMEN.

Nature and society lay a burden upon women, as the unwed woman, as the mate, as the vessel of hope, as parent when passing from hope to certainty, as the mother and nurse of the young. Thus, by Sema custom women must abstain " from the flesh of kites and hawks. Sometimes the reason given is that it causes unthrift, sometimes that it makes the woman who eats it too free with her nails, making her unpleasantly addicted to biting and scratching . . . women may not eat of the goat for fear of becoming libidinous, nor of chickens that lay here and there in different places lest they should become unfaithful and light of love. They may not eat either of any animal that dies in giving birth (no doubt for fear that they should do likewise) or of the flesh of any animal killed by a wild beast " (**18**). The list of foods genna for Angamis is long and interesting, and similar to the Sema rules (**19**). Among the Tangkhul Nagas " In some villages, such as those in which the cloth-weaving industry is carried on, unmarried girls are not permitted to eat dog or the flesh of any male animal " (**20**). Women in hope are still further beset by limitations on their diet, as well as on their domestic activities, since, as among the Khasis, she may not " finish any sewing she may have commenced before she became *enceinte* " (**21**), or as among the Anal she may not eat " chillies or honey " (**22**), while the Nagas forbid her the flesh of " bear or of any animal that has died a natural death " (**23**). A Kuki tribe, the Kolhen, " prohibit her from killing a snake, attending a funeral ceremony, and eating a crab and a certain vegetable called *chak* in its young state" (**24**). Perhaps they are forbidden to kill snakes for the reason given by the Semas and Tangkhuls (**25**) that the child might be "born with a tongue quivering in and out like a snake."

During her time of hope a woman among the Tangkhul Nagas can only wash her feet and hands; she may not take wild plantain fruit lest she die in child-birth, the result of the twisted bunches of the fruit; she may not gather burnt wood from the jungle lest the child be born coal black, nor carry any sharpening stone to the fields lest the child be born without hands or legs; she may not kill frogs for the frog is like a human being with hands and legs and fingers and toes, and must not be harmed (**26**).

TABUS ON MEN.

So, too, for men, as male, as unmarried, as married, as aged, as warrior, as hunter, parent, there are special rites, special duties, special disabilities. Among the Semas the food prohibitions fall "into two distinct classes, that of the animals, the flesh of which is not eaten because of some habit of the animal which inspires disgust for its flesh, and those the flesh of which is not eaten for fear of the consequences entailed by eating it. . . . In regard to the latter class of food gennas among the Semas it is to be noticed that the ill consequences which are held to follow the use of certain animals and birds as food more often attend the offspring of the eaters than the eaters themselves, and these foods, therefore, can be eaten by old or childless men who have no prospect of bringing more children into the world." The flying squirrels are "idiot," and "the eaters would therefore be liable to beget idiot children." Men who eat the crow pheasant "are liable to get cut up by their enemies, and young men will not eat it." Again, "if the spoon breaks with which the cooked rice is being taken from the pot, males may not eat of that rice (except the very old and practically bed-ridden). If this prohibition were not observed and the eater were at any time to run, he would get a stitch of violent and appalling severity, as though a piece of broken bamboo spoon were piercing his vitals, while if he were so naughty as to lick a chilli pestle, he would be haunted on the march by a noise just behind him, as of a pestle thumping on the mortar. Again he may not eat of a chicken that impales iteslf on a spear when flying from its roost in the house, for this would render him liable to slip and fall on his own spear " (**27**).

Much liberty is allowed to the unmarried in the matter of food, but with the Naga (**28**) as with the Kol, marriage marks a definite stage in social progress with the imposition of the full disabilities of tribal life. " So darf ein Kind, selbst bis zum Alter seiner Verheiratung, essen was Fremde ihm reichen, ohne seine Zugehörigkeit zu seinem Volke zu verlieren " (**29**).

Of the rites which the social sense demands of men as males, illustration may be given from the Angamis who for the due and adequate performance of the Derochu sickness genna kill a pig and " two chaste unmarried boys, one a Pezoma and the other a Pepfuma (Pezoma and Pepfuma are the names of the two moieties of Angami social structure), are sent into the jungle to bring a bit of tree to make a wood hearth, some firewood and some wormwood." They make fire, kill the pig, etc., and then " eat with the household and observe the same *kenna*. . . . In the evening the two boys are allowed to go " (**30**). The unmarried Oraons perform a rite each year in order to secure an increase of male children and good luck hunting (**31**). In the case of Khonoma and of most Eastern Angami villages the unmarried man wears a different cloth " (**31a**).

Among the Old Kuki clans in Manipur, there are rites

when the dual structure of some of the villages is specially marked by a rope-pulling ceremony as " marriages are only allowed between the young people who pull on the same side with the exception of the Chongthu who, being of the chief's family, may marry a girl of any family except their own " (**32**). There are rites, too, when " the unmarried girls take a prominent part " (**33**) rites at which " all the men attend but no women " (**34**), rites when the " young men and girl dance and drink together " (**35**).

In Mandla, in the Central Provinces " the Gonds still perform, or did till recently, various magical or religious rites to obtain success in fishing and hunting. The men of the village were accustomed to go out fishing as a communal act. They arrived at the river before sunrise and at midday their women brought them pej or gruel. On returning the women made a mound or platform before the house of the principal man of the party. All the fish caught were afterwards laid on this platform, and the leader then divided them, leaving one piece on the platform. Next morning this piece was taken away and placed on the grave of the leader's ancestor. If no fish were caught on the first day the women took the men no food. And if they caught no fish for two or three days running, they went and dug up the platform erected in front of the leaders' house and levelled it with the ground. Then the next morning early all the people of the village went to another village and danced the Sela dance before the tombs of the ancestors of that village. . . . . The Sela dance is danced by men alone. When a single Gond intends to go out hunting in the forest, he first lights a lamp before his household god in the house or if he has no oil he will kindle a fire, and the lamp or fire must be kept burning all the time he is out. . . . A Gond never takes food in the morning before going out hunting, but goes out in a fasting condition, perhaps in order that the god, seeing his hunger, may send him some game to eat. Nor will a Gond visit his wife the night before he goes out hunting" (**36**).

Thus, for the hunter and warrior, phases of male activity closely akin, there are special rules separating him from his wife when preparing for or returning from an expedition. Should a Naga bee hunter neglect the rule, for " any mistake leads to fearful stinging " (**37**), he is also " liable to be killed by enemies, and before the bee hunters leave their houses early in the morning to secure the best, nothing whatever must be taken out of the house. Should a domestic animal give birth to young, or a fowl hatch chickens within three days of going to take bees, the owner cannot go " (**38**). When a Tangkhul is about to make salt, he is separated from his wife (**39**), and no Sema woman may weave while her man is away hunting, fighting or trading. " If this prohibition were not observed, the husband will get his legs caught in a tangle of creepers when going through the jungle and thus meet with an accident " (**40**). Again, " should a man light his pipe at a fire on which a woman is dyeing thread, he becomes a weakling and turns black in complexion " (**41**). From the Angami area comes the account how, " In the matter of dress, we may compare the genna which forbids a man who has not taken a head to wear the hornbill's feather, the insignia of the successful warrior, with the genna which prohibits a man from not merely putting on, but even laying across or against, his body a petticoat which has once been worn by a woman " (**42**).

Ere a child is born, his father is, among the Khasis, not allowed to thatch the ridge of the house or to put handle to dao or axe (**43**). A Lushai will not cut open any animal that has been killed or cut off its limbs for fear lest his child be born without those limbs ; he believes, too, that if he takes the flesh of any wild beast found dead, his child will be still-born ; if he gives away any article of clothing to a man of a distant village, the child's health will be permanently impaired ; he also avoids hard work, because his performance of hard work–is considered to be injurious to the child's health " (**44**). All through the Naga area are similar customs on the birth of a child, indeed on the birth of any domesticated animal within the house (**45**). For the first ten days after a child is born to him a Maram Naga " must not go out in a high wind or cloudy weather for fear that the Wind God might injure the child " (**46**). For the first seven days " after a child's birth its spirit is supposed not to be quite at home in the little body and to spend some of its time perched like a bird on the parent's bodies and clothes, and therefore, for fear of injuring it, the parents keep as quiet as possible for these seven days " (**47**). Five to ten days after the child is born its body is said to be covered with small pimples, its lips become black and its strength decreases. The family then obtain a particular kind of creeping plant called Vawm, which they make into a coil. In the evening everything in the house that has a lid or covering is uncovered, and the child is passed thrice through this coil, which act is supposed to clear the child's skin and restore its strength. After this is finished, the parents go to bed and the pots or other receptacles are covered again by any of the other members of the family. The parents themselves must not replace any of these lids for fear that they might shut up the spirit of the child in them " (**48**). A Lamgang father may not eat of chicken for five days, but his wife is not restricted as to her diet (**49**). Of the curious custom known as the "*couvade*" there are notable instances in India.

Many come from a level of society above that with which we are concerned, evidence of the strength and persistency of the sentiments and beliefs of earlier days (**50**).

Age brings some release from the restrictions laid on vigorous manhood, but has its appointed tasks and responsibilities. Angamis consider it " improper for any but old men to make " the wooden dolls, some of which are elaborate and well dressed (**51**). There is here, too, an interesting genna at which the old men, when participating at a genna for the acquisition of social rank, may drink from leaves only (**52**). At Khonoma there is " a genna for stopping rain which has results out of all proportion to its simplicity, if, indeed the full rite has been revealed, which is perhaps unlikely. All that is said to be necessary is for a man who has had no children to take a dish of water and evaporate it out of doors by boiling it. When dry, he must say " Let the days be fine like this," and no rain will fall for seven years " (**53**).

Among the Anal " the first stones and earth are placed in the grave by aged men " (**54**) and the grave is dug " in case of unnatural death only by old grey-headed " men " (**55**) So too among the Tarau " Women dying in childbirth are buried by old men who have no further hope of becoming fathers, far from the village " (**56**).

There are yet other social groupings within these main bodies. Success in the chase or war, success in love, the due performance of a series of sacrifices, entitles the warrior or lover or social aspirant to display on his person or about his house the insignia of his achievements in these varied fields of human activity. The social order depends on the encouragement of marital ardour. Much might be said by way of criticism about a social order which kept the lads unwed till they could prove to the ladies of their choice their fitness for the estate of matrimony by securing somehow a human head. Moralists, too, are not ostentatiously ready to approve the religious sanction which opens the gate of a delectable heaven to gay Lotharios. Among the Lushais, to become a Thangchhuah, to be entitled to wear a special kind of striped cloth, with turban and feather plume, to have a verandah at the back of his house, to have a window in his house and an additional shelf near his bed, glories terrestrial, and to attain to Pielral, a desirable place from which there is no return to the worries of this life ; in short, to reach a glory celestial, it is necessary to kill certain animals or provide expensive sacrifices or achieve conspicuous success in the Courts of Venus (**57**). Nor are these ideas confined to the Lushais for among the Nagas of Chakrima and Kezama, custom has crystallised into a convention and the man who has to his credit a successful intrigue with a married woman living with her husband, may wear a fourth line of cowries on his kilt, an emblem which, in the bad old days, signified a head. The same badge of honour is worn by the man who has to his score success with two unmarried girls. The comparative scale is instructive (**58**). Nor is this all, for at the feet of statues of the dead erected by the grave are placed stones with faces carved on them for the enemies he had killed, and plain stones for the women he had loved (**59**).

SEX GROUPS.

Thus sex plays an important part in the economy of the lower culture. It affects social structure in the case of the Hill Kacharis who have " forty families or sects to which males may belong and 42 for females. The two extra in the latter case remain unaccounted for To give an example, one male sect is called Hasungsa and one female sect Sagaodi. A Hasungsa marrying a Sagaodi, the male issue are Hasungsas and the female Sagaodis " (**60**). It may be possible that some such idea underlies the Aimol custom by which at a ceremony, when the " thempu " invokes the spirit of the new-born child to take up its residence within the new-born infant " The name is given at the same time, the father's family choosing the name of a son and the mother's of a daughter " (**61**).

Much importance attaches in the lower culture to the " name." The significance and purpose from a social aspect of the rites by which the name is given to a "little stranger," shows clearly that in some cases it is definitely part of the Cycle of Life (**61**).

MARRIAGE GROUPS.

The sex grouping of the clans among the Hill Kacharis is most unusual, possibly unique. In other cases the children follow and belong to the clan of one or other of their parents and there are groups where, while the main line of descent is reckoned through one parent, there are social regulations affecting the individual, created by and resting on recognition of relationship through both parents.

With the Garos the system of matrilineal descent is clearly marked. Of the Santals we read that "He may marry into any other sept, including that to which his mother belonged . . . he may not marry into the sub-sept to which his mother belonged" (**62**), yet even here there is some, albeit slight, recognition of kinship through the mother in the bar against marriage into the mother's subsept. As typical of the order where matrilineal descent is primary and only secondary or minor effect is produced by the relationship through the father, I cite the Khasis, since they have a rule forbidding marriage with the daughter of the father's sister during the life-time of the father as well as a rule forbidding marriage with the daughter of his father's brother (**63**). Moreover, they have definite relationship terms, (*Dei Kha* and *Para Kha*) for male relations who may and may not marry and the term *Kha* means relation by male descent, while *Kur* is used for relatives on the mother's side. Then among such tribes as the Kukis and Lushai in recognition of kinship through the mother a fine is payable by the heir to her "*pu*" or protector on and by reason of her death (**64**).

Thus, always, everywhere, it would seem that the family (the adult woman with her dependent children, and the adult men who by social custom have marital access to her and the duty of protecting her), is primary and fundamental. It is a bilateral unit.

There has been of recent years important work on the Andamanese, which indicates that among them "A tribe is a loose aggregate, held together by a common dialect and vague feeling of kinship. It consists of local groups in no sense septs or clans, and these in turn of households, each of husband and wife with dependent immature children (**65**). Apparently there are cases of intermarriage between the local groups, especially where they come into contact and the practice of adoption which is common within the local group brings the groups closer together than would otherwise be the case (**66**).

A typical "tribe" in the lower culture is defined as a society speaking a common language, occupying in common a definite area, divided up into clans, which, again, are subdivided into families or households. As with Naga society the actual unit may be a village—not a tribe—since the language test fails and customs differ from village to village. The "tribe" may, and often does, regard itself as descended from a common ancestor. Community of descent is also often postulated for the clans, which, as a matter of fact, may be local groups of heterogeneous descent and not constituted by kinship real or fictive. As a rule, the reality of the kinship of the several members of the families or household is a matter capable of direct proof. Genealogical methods afford singular but convincing evidence of the nature of the bonds uniting these various divisions of society. There are exceptions, often most instructive, to generalisations, but, speaking generally, tribal feeling in the lower culture in India does not allow its women to go to other "tribes" for their husbands, nor does it exactly encourage, though it cannot always prevent, its men if they bring in women from other tribes to produce children are to be reckoned as members of the tribe. Within the tribe itself marriage is universal, compulsory on all those who reach or desire to reach social maturity. A superior social status attaches to the married and fertile over the unmarried as well as over the married but infertile, and benefits of a spiritual order accrue to those who have married and produced children. These are the methods of social coercion.

EXOGAMY : THE CLAN : DUAL ORGANISATION.

The marriage regulations rest almost universally on the law of exogamy which " is a common rule among savage and barbarous peoples never to marry a woman of their own tribal subdivision or group, but always to marry a woman of a subdivision or group different from their own " **(67)**. That rule means that there must be at least two subdivisions within the tribe, a form of social organisation which subsists in full vigour in two distinct tribes in India and was more widely spread because it is fundamentally and causally related to the classificatory system of relationship, of which there is abundant evidence in groups no longer constituted on the dual basis **(68)**. It is a positive rule, it is prospective for it settles the status of the issue.

A word as to the clan. " The *sib* (the clan of British anthropologists) is most briefly defined as a unilateral kinship group. The family is bilateral ; to say that an individual belongs to a certain family implies that he recognises relationship with a certain man as his father and a certain woman as his mother. The *sib* traces kinship through either parent to the total neglect of the other " **(68a)**. The discussion of social origins from which this quotation is taken is an admirable exposition of the views of an American expert who has handled field material and knows the rhythm of living structure. He recognises that the clan is only part and by definition a dependent part of a larger unit. So far as the lower culture in India is concerned the clans are exogamous, obliged, therefore, by their fundamental constitution to maintain relations with other, at least one other, similarly constituted exogamous clan. Thus membership of a clan, be it patrilineal or matrilineal, involves duties and responsibilities towards and relations with persons who are not members of the individual's own clan. True vision of the clan, what it is, what it does, in and for the social economy, can be secured only by viewing it as part of a whole, not as a self-contained, self-sufficient unit, in the air as it were. The classificatory systems of relationship include terms for members of the alien, as well as for the members of their own, clan. Thus in a matrilineal exogamous group with two clans, A and B, there are A men and A women, B men and B women. Any A man uses the term for " father " of an individual who is a member of the B clan, and the term for " father-in-law " of a member of A clan. In a patrilineal exogamous group with two clans any A man uses the term for " mother " of a woman of group B and the term for " mother-in-law " of a woman of group A. If analysis be succeeded by a synthesis which shall have regard to the whole society, the true nature and mode of function of the clan are evident ; it is one half of what in its simplest form is a bilateral or dual organisation. The symmetry of the dual structure ceases to be evident when the dual structure disappears or is replaced by a multiple order. Nevertheless each clan in a multiple group, one composed of any number of exogamous clans of similar constitution, has the characteristic of being incomplete as a true unit unless count be taken of its relations, its complementary relations, with the other clans. Symmetrical arrangements are found in societies which are organised on a multiple clan system. The vivid interest which social arrangements have for society is manifest in the order and method with which these relations are organised.

CASES OF DUAL ORGANISATION.

In the lucid account of the Tribes and Castes of the Central Provinces by the late Mr. R. V. Russell, it is stated that " The remains of a two-class system appear to be traceable among the Gonds of the Central Provinces. In one part of Bastar all the Gonds are divided into two classes without names, and a man cannot marry a woman belonging to a clan of his own class, but must take one from a clan of the other class. Elsewhere the Gonds are divided into two groups of six-god and seven-god worshippers among whom the same rule applies "**(69)**, and of their marriage rules and practices we are told that " The marriage of first cousins is considered especially suitable. Formerly, perhaps, the match between a brother's daughter and sister's son was most common . . . and the union of a brother's son to a sister's daughter has also become customary. The children of two sisters cannot, it is said, be married, and a man cannot marry his wife's elder sister, any aunt or niece, nor his mother-in-law or her sister. But marriage is not prohibited between grandparents and grandchildren. If an old man marries a young wife and dies, his grandson will marry her if she is of the proper age. In this there would be no blood relationship. . . . It is said that even among Hindu castes the grandfather will flirt with his grand-daughter and call her his wife in jest and the grandmother with her grandson. In Bastar a man can marry his daughter's daughter or maternal grandfather's or grandmother's sister. He could not marry his son's daughter or paternal grandfather's sister because they belong to the same sept as himself " **(70)**.

Again, " the smaller septs seem to serve no purpose for regulating marriage and to be no more than family names. The tribe might just as well be divided into two great exogamous clans only **(71)**." Apparently in " another part of Bastar there were found to be five classes and each class had a small number of septs in it. . . . . This class, A, had six septs, Class B five, Classes C and D one each, Class E four and Class F two. A man could not marry a woman of any sept belonging to his own class" (**72**).

From the Garos, a matrilineal people speaking a Tibeto-Burman language, inhabiting the hills immediately to the west of the Khasia Hills, comes evidence of a dual structure. They "are divided into two Katchis, or *phratries*, called *Marak* and *Sangma* (one of them has a third called *Momin*). A Marak may not marry a Marak, nor a Sangma a Sangma" (**73**). The Garo scheme is complete. If there be a cousin available, he is required to marry the youngest daughter, to live in his father-in-law's house and ultimately to marry his wife's mother who is also his father's sister. His father-in-law is also his mother's brother. If there be no cousin available, a man is selected called the *nokrom* or pillar of the house, who marries the daughter, lives in the house, and has to marry the widow. If there be neither cousin nor nokrom, the law of *Akim* obliges the clan to which the deceased man belonged to select a man of that clan to be the consort of the widow, for the sake of the interest of the clan, which had thus an interest in and exercised a dual control over the property (**74**). It is through the widow that succession to the property is effected, for, as Colonel Dalton states, "Inherent in males there is no right to succeed to any property of any description, and this is all to secure a transmission of pure blood; but though a son cannot inherit his father's property, his mother cannot be ejected from the position she enjoyed conjointly with her husband. The successor must recognise in her the mistress of the house, not only as his mother-in-law, should she stand in that relation to him, but also as his wife, though the marital rights be shared with her own daughter" (**75**). If a woman refuses to marry her nephew and marries another man, the nephew is entitled to compensation from both of them. Thus in so far as the succession to property is concerned, it is clear that the only way to enjoyment of the property is by marriage with the widow, who is often both the mother of the man's wife and the sister of the man's father.

As the law of *Akim* shows, the clans are complementary, each to the other, and together form a definite whole.

The Lonte have two, only two, exogamous divisions—Lanu and Changom (**75a**), and we are told that a Lonte girl's proper husband is her maternal first cousin. This is an obvious necessity in the circumstances of the case. The dual structure of the Kolhen tribe, one of the Old Kuki groups, described by Colonel Shakespear, is revealed incidentally at the " Keidun " festival, when the village is separated into two parties for the tug-of-war. " On one side are all the young men of the khul-lakpa's family—viz., the Chongthu—and on the other those of the Jete, to which the luplakpa belongs. With the Chongthu pull the young men of the following families—viz., Tulthung, Maite, Tiante, Laishel, Songchungnung, while with the Jete are associated the young men of the Lunglai, Rembual, Mirem, Tumtin and Vanbie. The girls of each family pull on the opposite side to the young men of their family. . . . Marriages are only allowed between the young people who pull on the same side, with the exception of the Chongthu, who, being of the chief's family, may marry a girl of any family except their own " (**76**). Clearly, then, we have two divisions, and a chief's family above, taking its wives from the other two groups. Here, as with the Garos, membership of the two main groups regulates marriage.

OTHER DUAL GROUPINGS.

The Angami have two main divisions, *Kepezoma* and *Kepepfuma*, so distinct that at the Derochu genna, " two chaste unmarried boys, one a Pezoma and the other a

Pepfuma," are brought into the ceremony for an active share (77). Elsewhere in this area, I found that "In nearly every Tangkhul village we find two village officers, the khullakpa and the luplakpa. In the village of Liyai in the Mao group, we have two pairs of exogamous divisions, with a prohibition against the intermarriage of the members of the paired clans. The Mao group is internally divided into two groups, the cause of their separation being, according to tradition, religious rather than social. The groups intermarry, it is true, but not to any great extent. At Maram there are two *khullakpas*, who are both under the same extended range of prohibitions. The Kabui tribe, according to Colonel McCulloch consists of two divisions, Songboo and Pooeron. . . . The Marrings again possess two divisions, Saibu, the elder, and Marring, the younger, which do not intermarry" (78). Further examination of this particular area brings out the facts that "Shongashon has four khel grouped in two exogamous pairs. Kalanamei has six khels; 1 and 2 form an exogamous group, and 4, 5 and 6 another; number 3 intermarries with both groups. The other three villages are divided into khels, which are exogamous, but are not grouped. Maram has three khels, which are exogamous, and two of them form an exogamous group" (79). The whole of this area is occupied by tribes whose traditions point to the existence of a dual organisation. Still some at least of these curious combinations may be the result of accretion of migratory groups, which joined with existing groups, so that—as local legends assert—the village has a multiple origin.

There are among the Khasias States which have two chiefs, a White and a Black Siem, and examination of the terms of relationship and the present conditions and prohibitions affecting marriage among the Khasias has led me to the opinion that the Khasis were at one time organised on a dual basis. When this social scheme was broken up either by internal growth and development or by external forces bringing in strangers as rulers, certain modifications of social structure were then effected which find preservation in the terms of relationship and in the new regulations prohibiting or restraining marriages on which the old order rested. It became necessary to make arrangements for giving wives to and taking wives from the new groups and the steps then taken separated them from an order still preserved among their neighbours the Garos (**80**).

Fuller and more penetrating inquiries may reveal features of social structure elsewhere which belong to and are survivals from an order based on simple duality of grouping.

The classificatory system of relationship holds among the Dravidian-speaking peoples among the Munda groups of Chota Nagpur, and modes of it, with variations due to local conditions, are certainly found in Assam. Whatever may be its significance its principles are derived, can be derived only from duality of social structure.

COUSIN-MARRIAGES.

Much importance attaches to the custom of marriage with a first cousin, the daughter either of a mother's brother or of a father's sister, but especially with the daughter of a mother's brother, which, as Sir James Frazer remarks, " has been, as a rule, permitted, and even favoured among all races except the Aryan " (**81**) in India. A man has, or may have, four female first cousins, the issue of his father's brother, of his father's sister, of his mother's brother and of his mother's sister. In a society constituted on the basis of exogamy with matrilineal descent, the issue of his mother's sister will be forbidden to him. In a society constituted on the basis of exogamy with patrilineal descent, the issue of his father's brother will be forbidden to him. In a society composed of only two exogamous divisions, not only will the issue of his father's brother be forbidden, but the issue of his mother's sister will also be forbidden, so that the only marriageable cousins will be the issue of his father's sister or of his mother's brother. These marriageable cousins are called cross-cousins and distinguished from the unmarriageable cousins whom Sir James Frazer calls ortho-cousins. It is not fair, though necessary from considerations of economy of space, to select passages from the long, thorough and scientific account of cross-cousin marriage in India and elsewhere given by Sir James Frazer (**82**) since the account should be studied as a whole, but I venture to call special attention to his finding that "the dual organization . . . was the source both of the systematic preference for the marriage of cross-cousins and of the systematic prohibition of the marriage of ortho-cousins" (**83**), and that "so far as the imperfect evidence at our disposal permits us to judge, the two areas (of cousin marriage and the dual organisation) appear to coincide exactly." To compare the tribes discussed in regard to the dual organisation, we find that "When a Gond wants to marry his daughter, he first looks for a husband among his sister's children, as it is considered the proper thing for first cousins to marry whenever such an arrangement is possible, though, strange to say, the rule is only thought absolutely binding where the brother's child happens to be a girl and the sister's a boy" (**84**). The matrilineal Garos practise cross-cousin marriage in a most notable form (**85**), (**86**), (**87**).

INTERMEDIATE CASES OF SYMMETRICAL OR SYSTEMATIC OR SPECIFIC EXOGAMY.

I turn now to an interesting class of cases which seem to be intermediate between the dual order (with its subdivisions) and the multiple or free order. As recorded by Colonel Shakespear (**88**) among the Tarau clan there are four families, and they marry thus: Pachana man marries Tlangsha girl; Tlangsha man marries Thimasha girl ; Thimasha man marries Khulpu-in girl and Khulpu-in man marries Pachana girl.

By this rule a Pachana always marries a Tlangsha woman so that a Pachana son will marry a Tlangsha daughter, the daughter of his mother's brother, or a woman of that status by the classificatory principle.

A Pachana girl must marry a Khulpuin man. Every Khulpuin man's mother was a Pachana woman. Therefore a Pachana marries a man who is actually or is classed as the son of her father's sister. Therefore a Pachana woman calls her husband's mother by the term used for her father's sister. Hertz records a similar grouping among the Kachins (**89**) ; Marip gives girls to Maran, who marry with N'Khum, also its girls go to Lepai, who marry Lahtawng, and their daughters are the wives of the Marip. It is thus intelligible that later accounts should display the Kachins as having the " general rule that a man should marry a first cousin on the female side, or, more precisely, the daughter of a mother's brother " (**90**).

Of the Chawte (**91**) Colonel Shakespear notes that—

A Marem lad may only marry a Makhan girl,
A Makhan lad may only marry an Irung girl,
An Irung lad may only marry a Marem, Thao or Kiang girl,
A Kiang lad may only marry a Makhan or Marem girl,
A Thao lad may only marry a Makhan girl.

It will be observed that a Marem lad may only marry a Makhan girl, but the Marem girls get spouses from Irung and Kiang, clans from which their brothers do not get wives. Thao gets wives from Makhan and gives girls to Irung but has no relations with the others. Irung gets wives from Marem, Thao and Kiang and gives girls only to Makhan, while Makhan gets wives only from Irung, but gives to Marem, and Kiang. Thus all clans give girls to clans from which they do not get wives. Thao is irregular.

Information has been sent to me from the Manipur Durbar which, compared with that published in the Burma Census Report, 1911 (**92**) and Mr. Hutton's account of the Semas (**93**) indicates the linguistic expression of the relationship between the modes of social structure.

	Tarau[1]	*Kachin*[2]	*Sema*[3]	*Chawte*[4]
Mother's brother ...	Pu*te*[5]	Tsa	Ngu	Pu
Father's sister	Ni	Moigyi	Ni	Ni
Mother's brother's wife	Pi*te*	Ni	Za or Fu	Pi
Father's sister's husband	Marang	Ku	Chi	Rang
Husband's mother	Ni	Moi	Ni	Ni
Wife's father	Pu	Tsa	Ngu	Pu
Husband's father ...	Marang	Ku	Ngu	Arang
Wife's mother	Pi	Ni	Ni	Pi

An early authority quoted by Sir James Frazer (**94**) describes the "Nagas of Assam" as practising cousin marriage and preferring the daughter of the mother's brother. Precisely to what Naga tribe this applied is not stated, but we know that among the Sema Nagas, "If otherwise suitable, marriage with the mother's brother's daughter or father's sister's son is preferred" (**95**). Among the Semas, as among other Naga tribes, the greatest respect is enjoined on a man

[1] From Manipur Durbar.
[2] Burma Census Report, 1911, Appendix B. xiii.
[3] Hutton's *The Semas*, pp. 140, 141.
[4] From Manipur Durbar.
[5] *Te* is a plural form.

for his mother's brother (**96**), and while "There is no social penalty attaching to the breach of this etiquette, the breach is believed to entail its own penalty of serious misfortune or death." There are definite obligations of gifts and returns between a man and the husband of his sister's daughter. A "Sema may marry his father's wife, other, of course, than his own mother, after his father's death" (**97**). One and the same term, *Aza*, is used for mother, for mother's sister and for the mother's brother's daughter, as if indicating that as a man may marry a woman having the status of mother as well as a woman having the status of mother's brother's daughter, so that the same term is applied to them both, as well as to the mother's sister, since "the vast majority hold that a man may marry his mother's sister by the same father and mother without any suggestion of impropriety" (**98**). But by preference they marry their mother's brother's daughter (**99**), so that one and the same term (*Angu*) is naturally used for mother's brother and wife's father.

FREE EXOGAMY.

Many are the tribes which are in the stage of free exogamy with special "local" rules to prevent marriages which may be deemed too close. How close, according to our ideas, marriages can be and yet be permitted, even encouraged, may be seen by some well-known cases. An Ernadan used to take his eldest daughter as his second wife (**100**). A Sema may marry his father's widow (not being his own mother), or his mother's sister (**101**). A Garo must marry his wife's mother when the latter becomes a widow in order to enjoy the property, and his wife's mother is naturally often his father's sister (**102**). A Kuruba may marry his elder sister's daughter (**103**). A Gond may marry his grand-daughter (**104**). But the principle of exogamy is still observed for the women belong to a group other than that of their husband's. It is not individual kinship, but membership of a definite group which regulates marriage. The groups are as wheels with individuals as cogs and the motion of the wheels is transmitted through the engagement of the cogs. The fact is that status, as Sir Henry Maine (**105**) pointed out long ago is the mark of societies in the lower culture. Status is a matter of the rights and duties of members of a group as such to one another, and to members of a similar group as such. Marriage rules are essentially matters of group relations. Both individuals as individuals, and groups as groups, are affected by marriage, and the fundamental reason is that group consciousness is stimulated by individual action. The group marriage question I do not propose to discuss.

As Lowie shows (**106**) "Sex moieties, divisions on the basis of matrimonial status, social clubs, secret fraternities, all criss-cross the bonds of the family and the *sib*, creating new units of incalculable significance for the individual's social existence. These 'associations' exist simultaneously. Their interests may conflict, may be independent, separable and distinct, may be combined and harmonised, and in the vast range and variety of institutions beliefs and customs may be found evidence of the phases of conflict, compromise, interaction and harmonisation by co-ordination with some central dominant social idea."

I cannot stay to describe the modes of exchange, of purchase, of servitude, nor the strange rites and practices which gather round marriage, that social process by which an individual forms a partnership with an individual of the opposite sex so that a family is started, a new social, economic and biological unit. As we see it, this process is conditioned by rules and regulations which are partly social, partly economic, partly biological. The rites marking this process in its stages are therefore of a similarly varied nature. Some refer distinctly to the biological aspect of the process ; others are significant of the economic importance: the purely social factors—the modification of status, immediate and prospective, the accretion of a new unit—are evident. To understand the process adequately, the effects of the several factors must be ascertained, simply at first, then in combination and in combined interaction. The future effects of the process, the status of the issue, the economic adjustments are clearly contemplated and provided for by the rules and the rites which are valid and observed only because they rest on the authority of society. What ideas, what imaginings, lie behind the authority of society can often be divined only with difficulty. Marriage is essentially a process envisaging definite problems, prospective of issue, regulating the social status of that issue, regarding that issue as the reincarnation of deceased members of the group. Thus for me the whole mass of marriage rules and rites is dominated by, and intelligible as a whole, only if regarded as organised in relation to the concept of society as composed of ever-changing, ever-recurring, units of a living organism of complex and varied, every-varying, structure, to be viewed as we are asked to view life itself, where "en réalité le corps change de forme à tout instant. Ce qui est réel, c'est le changement continuel de forme : la forme n'est qu'un instantané pris sur une transition." (**107**).

1. *Rites de Passage*, p. 97.
1a. *Primitive Societies* (Lowie), p. 324; *Anthropology* (Marett), p. 243.
2. *Lushei Kuki Clans*, p. 55.
3. *Sema Nagas*, p. 51 *n*.
4. *Ibid.*, p. 54.
5. *Popular Religion and Folklore of Northern India*, i. 69. J.R.A.I., xlix., pp. 237 *sq*.
6. *The Oraons*, p. 272 *et seq*.
7. *Gebiet das Kols Mission*, p. 65.
8. *Naga Tribes of Manipur*, p. 168.
9. *The Angami Nagas*, pp. 197, 204.
10. *Ibid.*, p. 199.
11. *Ibid.*, p. 205.
12. *Lushei Kuki Clans*, p. 152.

13. *Ibid.*, p. 19.
14. *The Khasis*, p. 190.
15. *The Garos*, p. 147.
16. *Practical Handbook of Kachin* (H. F. Hertz), p. 130.
17. *Rites de Passage*, pp. 88 *sq.*, 67 *n.* See Lowie, *Primitive Society*, pp. 102, 250.
18. *The Semas*, p. 95.
19. *The Angami Nagas*, p. 94.
20. *The Naga Tribes of Manipur*, p. 182.
21. *The Khasis*, p. 160.
22. *The Lushei Kuki Clans*, p. 160.
23. *The Naga Tribes of Manipur*, p. 182.
24. *The Lushei Kuki Clans*, p. 160.
25. *The Sema Nagas*, p. 90 *n.* Census Report, 1911, vol. iii., p. 76.
26. Census Report, 1911, vol. iii., *loc. cit.* *Cf. Folklore of the Santal Parganas* p. 415.
27. *The Sema Nagas*, p. 95.
28. *The Naga Tribes of Manipur*, p. 78
29. *Gebiet das Kols Mission*, p. 88 ; see p. 62.
30. *The Angami Nagas*, p. 234.
31. *The Oraons*, pp. 225, 239.
31a. *The Angami Nagas*, p. 26.
32. *The Lushei Kuki Clans*, p. 167.
33. *Ibid.*, p. 168.
34. *Ibid.*, p. 168.
35. *Ibid.*, p. 169.
36. *Tribes and Castes of the Central Provinces*, iii. 107.
37. *The Angami Nagas*, p. 236.
38. *The Sema Nagas*, p. 72.
39. *The Angami Nagas*, p. 71.
40. *The Sema Nagas*, p. 51.
41. *Ibid.*,
42. *The Angami Nagas*, p. 191.
43. *The Khasis*, p. 160.
44. Census Report, 1911, vol. iii., p. 140.
45. *The Naga Tribes of Manipur*, p. 177.
46. Census Report, 1911, vol. iii., p. 77.
47. *The Lushei Kuki Clans*, p. 81.
48. Census Report, 1911, vol. iii., p. 140.
49. *The Lushei Kuki Clans*, p. 162.
50. *Ethnographic Notes in Southern India*, pp. 547–551.
51. *The Angami Nagas*, p. 67.
52. *Ibid.*, p. 231.
53. *Ibid.*, p. 236.
54. *The Lushei Kuki Clans*, p. 164.
55. *Ibid.*, p. 165.
56. *Ibid.*, p. 174.
57. Census Report, 1911, vol. iii., p. 141, and *Lushei Kuki Clans*, p. 62.
58. *The Angami Nagas*, p. 25.
59. *Ibid.*, illustrative note, p. 227.
60. Soppitt, *Account of the Kachari Tribes*, p. 36

61. *Lushei Kuki Clans*, p. 161.
62. *Tribes and Castes of Bengal*, ii., 227–228.
63. *The Khasis*, p. 78.
64. *Lushei Kuki Clans*, pp. 51, 82, 86, 199.
65. Hartland, *Primitive Society*, p. 28.
66. Census Report, 1901, vol. iii., p. 51; *cf.* Brown, *Andaman Islanders*, p. 73.
67. Frazer, *Totemism and Exogamy*, vol. iv., p. 72.
68. Frazer, *Folklore of the Old Testament*, vol. ii., p. 223, 227. *sq.*
68a. Lowie, *Primitive Society*, p. 105.
69. *Tribes and Castes of the Central Provinces*, vol. i., p. 144.
70. *Ibid.*, vol. iii., p. 71.
71. *Ibid.*, vol. iii., p. 65.
72. *Ibid.*, p. 65.
73. Census Report, 1911, vol. i., p. 253.
74. *The Garos*, pp. 68, 69, 72, 73.
75. *Descriptive Ethnology of Bengal*, p. 63.
75a. *The Kuki Lushei Clans*, p. 173.
76. *The Kuki Lushei Clans*, p. 167.
77. *The Angamis*, pp. 110, 234.
78. *The Naga Tribes of Manipur*, p. 74 *sq.*
79. *The Angamis*, pp. 117, *n.*, 361.
80. *Man in India*, vol. i., pp. 106–127.
81. *Folklore of the Old Testament*, ii., p. 134.
82. *Ibid*, pp. 96–371.
83. *Ibid.*, p. 240.
84. *Gazetteer of the Central Provinces*, p. 276,
85. *The Garos*, p. 58.
86. Census Report, 1891, vol. i., 229.
87. *Man in India*, vol. i., pp. 106–127.
88. *The Lushei Kuki Clans*, p. 173.
89. *Handbook of Kachin Grammar*, p. 140.
90. *Gazetteer of Upper Burma*, vol. i., part 1, p. 404.
91. *The Lushei Kuki Clans*, p. 154.
92. Census Report, 1911, vol. ix., p. lxxiii.
93. *The Sema Nagas*, pp. 140, 141.
94. *Folklore of the Old Testament*, ii., 133.
95. *The Sema Nagas*, p. 132.
96. *Ibid.*, p. 137.
97. *Ibid.*, p. 136.
98. *Ibid.*, p. 131.
99. *Ibid.*, p. 132.
100. *Castes and Tribes of S. India*, vol. ii., p. 217.
101. *The Sema Nagas*, p. 136.
102. Census Report, 1891, vol. i., p. 229.
103. Ethnographical Survey of Mysore, *Bulletin* 1, p. 8.
104. *Tribes and Castes of the Central Provinces*, vol. iii., p. 72.
105. *Ancient Law*, p. 170.
106. *Primitive Society*, p. 283.
107. Bergson, *Evolution Creatrice*, p. 327.

LECTURE V.

The Cycle of Life—Birth and Name-giving Rites—Initiation and Puberty Rites—The Educational System—Marriage—Social Distinctions—Death and Mortuary Ritual—Re-incarnation Beliefs—The Origin of Death—Religious Beliefs—The Nature of the Soul—Causes of Death —Treatment of Sickness—Man and Nature—Totemism—The Lower Culture as the Matrix of Higher Culture.

I propose to trace the life history, briefly, of individuals as they pass from stage to stage of their career in the social group of which they are members. The first rite is that by which a name is given to the infant. It is well agreed that " Names also are regarded as concrete . . . as part of the person or thing to which it was applied, and containing part of his life " (**1**) More than that it is the part of him which is his soul. The rites of name-giving are a social act by which the child is made an individual, and is brought into a group, be it small or large. Thus with the Garos " The child is nearly always named after an ancestor who has been dead for some years. The name of a living relative or of one who has recently died is never given (**2**). By the Kabui Nagas " names are not given at random, but are compounds of the father's and grandfather's names or those of other near relations " (**3**). There are name cycles which may conceal a personal name and are certainly supplemented by nicknames (**4**). But there are other means to hand by which the name may be ascertained. Dreams will help, and so the parents among some Nagas will " note " their dreams so that the name of their newborn child may be rightly chosen. Omens, too, are taken among the Khasis (**5**) as also among the Kols and Hos who call neighbours and relations together for the rite. " Es wird nicht ein beleibiger Name gewählt, sondern zuerst muss eine Art Orakel gefragt werden-und nur wenn dieses schweigt, wird ein Name gewählt. Das Orakel besteht darin, dass ein Gefäss mit Wasser gefüllt wird, In dieses Wasser wird bei Nennung des Namens ein Reiskorn gewerfen ; sinkt es, dann wird dieser Name genommen, bleibt es auf der Oberfläche, wird er verworfen. Bei einem erstgeborenen Knaben werden die Namen des nachsten verstorbenen Verwandten gerufen, indem Glauben, dass vielleicht einer der selben aus der Unterwelt zuruckgekehrt und in dem kleinen Neugeborenen auss neue in diese Welt eingetreten sein konnte (**6**). By the Oraons the same method is employed, but the test lies in two rice grains meeting when a name is called. The names are called over in regular order. " First the paternal grandfather's name, then the paternal great grandfather, the father's, the paternal uncle's and the maternal grandfather, then the names of other relatives " (**7**). " The practice of naming children after ancestors," says the Bengal Census Report for **1911** (**8**), " also seems to point to a belief in the conservation of spirits in the same family. This is clearly expressed in the ceremony attending the naming of children among the Khonds. A *Guru* is called on the seventh day after its birth to discover by divination which of the ancestors has animated the new-born child. . . . The Santals also name their children after ancestors. The eldest son takes the name of his paternal grandfather, a second son that of his maternal grandfather, a third son that of the paternal grandfather's brother, a fourth son that of the maternal grandfather's brother, etc. A similar custom is observed in the case of girls, the names relations on the female side being taken in the same order. Among the Bhuiyas the name of the grandfather is given to the eldest son, that of the great grandfather to the second son, and then the names of collateral relatives according to seniority." Sarat Chandra Roy makes it clear that " for the Bhuiyas all the names taken must be those of deceased relations, for the child is supposed to be the reincarnation of some dead relatives " (**9**). The little stranger is no stranger but he must be identified.

There may be other motives at work as in the Sema custom, where he " never gives to the child the name of a living relation, though the names of dead ancestors are popular among those with a child to name." The explanation given is that, if the name of a living senior be given the elder will die, as a substitute for him in this world has been provided. Possibly there is behind this some fear that such nomenclature would be tantamount to saddling one body with two souls, one of which being useless would die. The very strong objection which Semas have to having an animal named after them may be connected with the same idea. At the same time they do not appear to have, at the present time, any belief at all that the dead are reincarnated in the living " (**10**).

There follow then the domestic ceremonies when the first hair is cut, when the ears are bored, when the teeth are filed, when the tattooing is begun, when the maiden is known to be mature, ceremonies whose full and varied significance can be ascertained only by careful exploration of the " mixed motives " which influence the people who practise them. The Santals brand the young man on the left forearm, for " Unless these marks are fully visible when he comes to die, a terrible fate will befall him. As soon as the breath leaves his body, a large worm will burrow into his breast and slowly devour his body " (**11**). Among the Abors and Nagas tattooing has much the same purpose, " for thereby is provided a means of identification in the life hereafter " (**12**). As Dr. Thurston shows (**13**) vague ideas of hygiene may operate as well as aesthetic motives of self-adornment, but there is no doubt that the religious or traditional factor is most strong, involving complex associations which explain its wide validity. These mutilations serve to differentiate one group from another, to emphasise their unity with their fellows who practise the same rites.

In due course, after the years of dependence on the mother, whose part in the development of the mental capacities of the young is very great, the boy or girl will enter the "school," the Bachelor's Hall, or the Spinster's House, wherein they will receive an education of an entirely vocational nature, fitting them, be it admitted, rather well for the life that lies before them. Civics and crafts, to use the jargon now in vogue, form the substance of the training of these years. For some the "school period" will not cease till they enter the full life of the married, even in extreme cases, till a child is born to them. The rites of marriage, the preliminaries, the bargaining and the omen-taking, the conditions, physical and social regarded as proof of fitness for this estate, the complex ceremonies which remove the boy and girl from a stage of social tutelage to plenary social responsibility almost by violence, have been described in amplitude of detail by many skilful observers. The range of complexity is considerable. Simple cohabitation by mutual consent is accepted as "marriage" by the jungle tribes of Southern India such as the Chenchus and the Yanadis (**14**) or by the poorer Gonds (**15**). Among the Andamanese, "When the elders of a sept are aware that a young couple are anxious to marry, the bride is taken to a newly-made hut and made to sit down in it. The bridegroom runs away into the jungle, but after some struggling and pretence at hesitation, is brought in by force and made to sit in the bride's lap. This is the whole ceremony. The newly-married couple have little to say to, and are very shy of, each other for at least a month after marriage, when they gradually settle down together" (**16**). Indeed the marriage is not socially complete till a child has been born, since "In the case of a young married couple who are childless, if either die, the survivor is not the chief mourner and does not even assist at the obsequies which are performed solely by the relatives of the deceased (**17**). The long-drawn-out ceremonies of the Mundas and Santals who, nevertheless, recognise minor modes of marriage, include the rite known as Tree-marriage by which the bride and bridegroom are married to a mango or mahua tree. The sociological interest of this rite arises in part from the fact that it is an integral part of rites forming the main and most important of the marriage modes of these people. What does it mean, does it mean anything at all ? The votary of totemism.(**18**) sees in it a totemic rite, but these trees are not totems and the rite is universal, not confined to the clans which have totems and are the marriage units. It is said that it is an act of penance for a violation of communal rights (**19**), but exactly and in what matter the penitential aspect of the rite consists, is left obscure. A third explanation (**20**) is that it is a mock ceremony destined to baffle the vigilance of the evil spirits who are specially active on such solemn occasions, and to secure the lawlessness in success of the marriage. They take it in all seriousness, however, and in the explanation of the rite as a fertility rite, definite, concrete, specific (**21**), I see the history of it. Be it remembered that these are the fruit trees which play so important a part in the economics of these people, that as an intelligent Santal remarked to Sir William Hunter, " good men entered into fruit-bearing trees " (**22**) that the dead are reborn in the living, that no human marriage can take place till the bones of the dead of the year that is gone have been placed in the tribal ossuary, that man has two souls, one male and one female, and that, in the world hereafter, " All the spirits are employed in grinding the bones of past generations with a pestle made of the wood of the castor oil tree in order to provide the gods with a good supply of material to produce the children yet unborn " (**23**). The Kurubas erect the milk post at marriages for the definite purpose of "ensuring continuity of the line" (**24**). The purpose of all marriage rites is to ensure the continuity of the line, that is the constant succession of reincarnated souls, as the purpose of the name-giving rites is to ascertain which of the deceased ancestors has indeed returned.

SOCIAL DISTINCTIONS.

Prowess in war entitles the Naga to wear emblems, sometimes very unmistakeable emblems, of his efforts to reduce the enemy population. Performance of social rites, feasts to the village, sacrifices of valuable animals in prescribed and adequate quantity, are signalised by a "regular scale of cloths from which it can be told at a glance precisely to what status in the performance of such ceremonies the wearer has reached" (**25**). The sole advantage accruing in these days to the wealthy and ambitious Naga, who duly performs these expensive rites, is the privilege of distinctions in dress and domestic architecture. Among the Lushais the spiritual benefit of escape from the mortal coil of reincarnation can be assured by the due sacrifice of mythan on a series of occasions (**26**). To this is added the right of special clothes and of making improvements in the house. There is now apparently no mystery about these methods of achieving greatness. Stone monuments are viewed as memorials of the dead. I have reason to know that they are still erected by the living (**27**) and are associated with the belief in reincarnation. A Naga once complained in great distress of the action of the Public Works Department in breaking up his stone memorial as road metal, and on investigation I found that "the luck" of the whole family was associated with the stone whose extinction was thus threatened.

The attitude of the lower culture towards their dead and death is fully—often very clearly—displayed by the complexity and duration of the rites performed for the disposal of the human remains in which enter various elements in order to serve the many purposes involved by the relations of the dead to the living, by the nature of the relations of soul and body, by the relations of the individual with the social groups of which in life he was a member. As I see them, there are distinct principles at work. In both of them I see the influence of the belief in reincarnation. The married are distinguished from the unmarried for marriage is a condition precedent for re-incarnation. Hence those cases where the rites of marriage are performed over a dead bachelor or spinster in order that the formal status of married individual shall be theirs (**28**). I see, too, at work the principle of distinguishing between those whose manner of death indicates that they are for ever precluded from rebirth, and those who are liable to return. There are those who are favoured by fortune, who by their strong arm and swift skill, or by their depth of purse, have achieved greatness and freedom from return to this world of woe. Folk of quality are never damned. Besides those who have in these ways achieved greatness are those who are born great in those societies where a permanent social order and precedence have been established. These things count in the lower culture and have a value. For them all death is the occasion of social anxiety, for there is "something contagious about dying, and association with death is liable to cause it. Merely to spread an untrue report of a man's death may cause it in itself." Thus the Semas (**29**). It is, too, an occasion when there is evident a breach in the social fabric, a sense of communal as well as of personal and individual loss, a recognition of individuality in opposition to the solidarity of society. Thus it is common to find that an unnamed child is buried with scant ceremony, for it has never been, it can never be, admitted to society. From the moment of birth, by reason of the manner of the birth, there are children deemed unfit to live. Among the Pabri Bhuiyas should a child be born with one or more teeth, it is " generally suffocated and thrown into a stream " (**30**). At Phweelongmai in Manipur female infanticide was once common " caused by a superstition which condemned to death all such as were born in a particular position " (**31**).

It is recorded of the Angamis that " Infanticide used to be practised in the case of children born of unmarried girls. In such cases delivery had to take place in the jungle and the child was killed ; the Kezami women used further to pierce its feet all over with thorns to prevent its visiting and haunting the mother in her dreams. It was believed that if it was allowed to grow up the village would have no success in hunting or in war " (**32**). One of the strangest effects of the belief in reincarnation is that observed among the Khonds, who " believe that souls almost invariably return to animate human forms in the families in which they have been first born and received. But the reception of the soul of an infant into a family is completed only on the performance of the ceremony of naming upon the seventh day after its birth. The death of a female infant, therefore, before that ceremonial of reception, is believed to exclude its soul from the circle of family spirits, diminishing by one the chance of future female births in the family " (**33**). This belief, reported by an early observer, has been reinvestigated, and " Inquiry shows that there is no belief among the Khonds at the present time that the ceremony of receiving a child into the family on the seventh day after birth confers the privilege of re-entering the family at some future time. This power is acquired only when the child has become an adult and been married " and " souls of unmarried persons cannot enter the circle of family spirits " (**34**).

The Yerukalas of Nellore, in Madras, accord to the married the privilege of a bier while they carry the unmarried to the grave simply wrapped in a mat (**35**). Amongst the Marias, " who are probably the best type we possess of the primitive Gond, the dead are waked in the Irish fashion. . . . If the deceased was an adult male, the body is next secured to a Mahwa tree in an erect posture and then burned. . . . Children and women are always buried " (**36**).

But the most widely-spread source of variation in mortuary ritual is that which relates to the mode of death. Of the Old Kuki Clans, Colonel Shakespear states that "All these clans bury their dead in special cemeteries outside the village, and unnatural deaths or deaths in childbirth are universally considered that the deceased has failed in some way, and the corpses of such unfortunates are buried outside the cemetery and with scant ceremony. . . . The Anal makes a distinction between deaths in childbirth and deaths by accident or in war. In the former case the body is buried in the cemetery, the grave being dug by those of her household and food and drink and domestic utensils are deposited therein. The husband has to sacrifice a pig and feast the village before the burial and the village is " sherh " for that day. The first stones and earth are placed in the grave by aged men, and the filling then completed by young men. The thempu having muttered some charms, the young men and women sing and dance fōr the deliverence of the soul. In cases of ordinary death the grave is dug by men not of the household, but in case of unnatural death only old grey-headed men may perform the task, and the grave is dug in the jungle and no dance or song terminates the funeral, but the village is not " sherh." Of the belief that underlies and shapes these practices he tells us " The Anal Kolhen and Lamgang believe that after hovering around the grave for some time, the spirit is reincarnated in some new-born child, but that an unnatural death prevents this and the spirit passes away skywards and returns no more (**37**). Similar distinctions are found among the Angamis (**38**), and of the existence of the belief in reincarnation I can cite the evidence of an early record now some fifty years old (**39**). Of the Kols we find that " Anders aber verläuft diese Prozedur wenn ein Mensch eines unnaturlichen oder plötzlichen Todes stirbt, wie z.B. wenn einer erschlagen oder von Tiger zerrissen und getötet wird, wen jemand die gerichtliche Todesstrafe zu erleiden hat oder einer Amputation gesterben ist, oder auch wenn eine Frau bei der Geburt eines Kindes oder innerhalb von fünfzehn Tagen nach ihrer Entbindung im Wochenbett starb. Alle diese Unglücklichen können nicht verbrannt d-h nicht rite bestattet werden, weil sie nicht zu den pachbalar = den Vorfahren in der Unterwelt versammellt werden, sondern zu bösen Geistern geworden sind, die ihren Aufenthalt in der Luft, in Wäldern, Ruinen, Begräbnisplätzen, an öden Orten usw nehmen und durch blutige Opfer in Ruhe gehalten werden müssen. Ihnen kann nicht geholfen werden, man muss sich nur vor ihnen schützen. . . . Ein vom Tiger gefressener Mensch wird sogar selbst zum Tiger und der Ort wo das Unglück geschehen ist, muss in gleicher Weise ausgezeichnet werden, damit man nicht vom Tiger angefallen werde " (**40**).

The association of this sharp distinction between those who die an ordinary death who after death are joined to those that have gone before them to the underworld and those whose manner of death precludes them from peace among their fellows save at the price of special and bloody rites is as marked among the Dravidian speaking Oraons who knew them as Churil (ghost of women dying in childbirth) Bhula or wanderer (the ghosts of all " that have died an unnatural death ") (**41**) and Balsadhak a (stillborn child's ghost). Perhaps the most remarkable combination of funeral rites where both methods of classifying the dead, that is either by their social status or by the manner of the death, are in evident operation, is that afforded by the Killekyatas, as described in Mysore Ethnographic Survey, *Bulletin*, No. XXII. The dead are generally buried. Persons affected with such diseases as leprosy and also pregnant women are cremated, and the bodies of those meeting with unnatural death, such as from wild animals, are sometimes buried under stone heaps. The bodies of married persons are placed in a sitting, and those of others in a lying, posture in the grave. With them as with the Kols, Mundas, Santals, and the Old Kuki tribes, the cycle of belief and practice is complete, birth rites to name the child after a deceased relative, marriage rites to ensure "the continuity of the line" classification of the dead by social status and mode of death, belief that "their deceased ancestors, especially the married amongst them, always remain with them. The names of the departed should be given to children in the family."

It is the purpose of funeral rites to provide for souls of these diverse and difficult natures, to safeguard the living against the infection which is death, to repair the breach which private or individual misfortune or mistake has caused in the solid scheme of society. Thus are combined, now in one, now in a long series of rites, a variety of social purposes, a variety which is still further diversified, as we have seen, by beliefs as to the fate of those who die a blessed death, who are to return, whose rank and public spirit, as these things are judged in the lower culture, entitle them to spiritual benefits as well as to temporal distinction. Among the Nagas, the Old Kuki tribes and the Munda-speaking peoples, both the Khasias and the lowlier folk of the plateau of Chota Nagpur, is found a communal rite by which final rest is assured to the ghosts of those that have died a "good" death during the year

We have now to examine the beliefs current in the lower culture as to the nature of man, the origin and cause of death and sickness, the origin and nature of the world in which man lives, the nature of the Powers that made and rule that world. Here, as always, we must turn to the prominent features of the mental attitudes of the social consciousness of the lower culture as we have found them to be. There is, first, the special importance assigned to dreams which have not only reality but a degree of value exceeding the impressions of the waking state. It is true, too, as Mr. Russell has shown (**42**) that " the tendency to make everything concrete is a principal and salient characteristic of . . . primitive religion." Add to that the " tendency to coin a separate word for every individual conception " (**43**), with its necessary accompaniment of a " difficulty in forming words for abstract ideas," and we know the lines on which we can make real progress in our investigations.

Definition may be an essential element in dogma, but it is dangerous and misleading to define too rigorously or to dogmatise about the attitudes of the lower culture towards what we call the supernatural as distinguished from the natural as two separate, mutually exclusive categories. The classification is ours, not theirs. Mr. Hutton observes that, " In common with other savage races the Angami regards the supernatural in general from a point of view that is sublimely vague. . . . He has a very clear idea of how gods should be served, and that whoso serves them otherwise shall die, if not physically, at least socially. And this, although much of the service which he offers seems to be proffered to no god in particular, to no definite personal beings, but is associated merely with such supernatural forces as may influence his destiny or his daily life. At the same time, while he does not, like the civilised man, naturally classify and departmentalise his notions of the supernatural, he does recognise some sort of distinction between, on the one hand, souls of the dead (and perhaps of the living) and, on the other, deities (" *terhoma* ") of a more or less definite nature, ranging from deities with certain functions and individual names to vague spirits of the jungle, stone and stream (**44**)." There are gods, there are souls of the dead, there are forces which influence the ' destiny and daily life ' of men, there is service to be done in due order by men lest they perish in the flesh or be outcast by their fellows. As Sir James Frazer reminds us (**45**) " not least in the undeveloped savage religions . . . theory and practice fuse with and interact on each other too closely to be forcibly disjoined and handled apart." Since, however, definitions are necessary, if only because time is precious, we need not look for a definition of a God beyond that given by Sir James Frazer : " By a God I mean a beneficent supernatural spirit, the ruler of the world, or some part of it, who resembles man in nature though he excels him in knowledge and power." In a passage of profound analysis he finds " two sorts of gods whom man discovers or creates for himself by the exercise of his unaided faculties, to wit, natural gods whom he infers from his observation of external nature and human gods or inspired men whom he recognises by virtue of certain extraordinary mental manifestations in himself or in others (**46**). To these two classes he adds yet a third class, the deified spirits of dead men " (**47**). Thus if we adopt this classification as a working hypothesis of the origin of the principles of natural theology, as revealed in the acts and beliefs of the lower culture, Theoplasm is within man himself, is the very stuff and substance of his thoughts, is man himself.

The forces, social, environmental, natural, historical, which shape and mould and control and limit the thoughts of man, have operated as surely in this as in other directions of his activity. Yet throughout the lower culture we find not unity of belief not uniformity of attitude, but a general similarity of ideas on many points. Thus the Andamanese believe in a being named Puluga, or Bilika, who made earth and sky and sea, who with an associate named Tarai, produces rain, storms, thunder and lightning, whence arises a special relation in regard to fire. The very sex of this being is a matter on which the evidence seems to be inconclusive, while the nature of the being towards the activities of the Andamanese is shown by the anger displayed at melting or burning beeswax, cutting, digging up, or in any way interfering with a certain number of plants, particularly during a certain period of the year, and killing a cicada or making a noise during the time the cicadæ are singing at morning or evening" (**48**).

The Naga, like the Lushai, knows a Creator who is called Alhou by the Semas; Kepenopfü, a mother Goddess, ancestress of the Angamis; Kamyou by the Tangkhuls; Pathien by the Lushais and their congeners. It is clear that Kepenopfü—the Angami Ancestress, is nowadays being given a male character. Here and there, as with the Quoirengs, is a belief in a Creator deity named Kampinu, or the wife of Kampini, John Company, that distant, mysterious, powerful entity, in whose name strange men, few in number, ruled among them. Some of these High Gods indeed take but little care of the world they have fashioned or of the men that they have set to live therein, while others are as the "supreme dispenser of good and evil" (**49**). There are spirits of the jungle, of the sea where, as with the Andamanese, the sea is known in their daily life, of the stone and stream, spirits who give good crops, but must be kept in good temper, lest they destroy the labour of man's hands. Some are named, known, feared, propitiated. Many are without a name, somethings that work havoc and ruin. With the Oraons of Central India there has developed a hierarchy of spiritual powers with a correspondingly complicated organisation of human ministers to serve the Deotas, the Sun, the Earth, the clan village and family deities, the spirits of dead women, whose hope was shattered in them ere its dawn could be, of men killed in the jungles by a tiger, of all whose souls are denied rest with the fellowship of the glorious dead, of young bridegrooms snatched by death ere the prime of life, of all whose manner of death was strange, terrifying, memorable.

The social organisation makes due and adequate provision for the maintenance of relations with these powers. There are the official representatives of the community, the Naga Kemovo, the Lushai puithiam or wise man, the Oraon panch or sankatalas (**50**), the Santal and Munda Pahan. Immigrant communities enlist the services of a local expert as the Baiga who is a Kol in the employ of Oraon villages. The choice of these permanent civil servants is effected by heredity or by selective omens on proper principles, since they are the conservators of the traditions of diplomacy with the sacred powers. Here, again, the element of continuity is implemented by an element through which variations and adjustments to varying conditions are effected; for the *ojha* and the *thumomi* often employ means analogous with those of the official ritual, yet they are among Nagas "arrant frauds, and practise any sort of knavery that a gullible *clientele* finds attractive" (**51**). Persons who are subject to hypernormal or abnormal mental activities, women as well as men, old and young, become intermediaries between this and the other world. Some are born to this greatness and others acquire it by labour and long austerities and by payment of filthy lucre. Thus the Oraons know that the intensive course of training in these horrid arts lasts for but one year, and if by the end of that time she has filled her record (a hole in which a pebble is placed for each lesson learnt) "she has learnt everything. She has the power to take away life and to restore it. Otherwise, if she has only succeeded in partially filling the hole, she can only take away life" (**52**). The line which divides the sacred from the profane may be drawn sharply in theory, in the study of the scientist, but in actual life it is uncertain, vague and inconstant. Things and persons that are at one moment highly sacred, endued with strange qualities, with mysterious power to bless and blast, to hurt and to heal, to help and to harm, are at other moments—fortunately

—ordinary creatures of flesh and blood, ordinary things available for common use. Yet all that is useful is sacred, somewhere, some time, because it is useful and ministers to some need, social or other. There come upon them influences which give rise to the beliefs in possession, in second sight, in occult relations with forces capable of yielding what is needed. Society believes in them, in their powers, invests them with authority, uses them and destroys them when it is moved against them. Yet there is always an element in society which is permanently marked off as the official representative of society, protected by tabus, by special rules of food, dress, behaviour and language. There are things, there are events, which are viewed as always charged with divine power, fraught with mystery, dangerous, holy. It is of the essence of religion from a social aspect that the moments or crises of social life—birth, marriage, sickness, death—when the individual emerges from and stands forth in contrast, in opposition, to his group, that the manifestations of the powers and forces considered sacred are most conspicuous and at the height of their activity. Excite society into activity by the reaction of an individual, and the real nature of religious forces, as of social origin, is revealed immediately.

" European philosophers," we are told by competent authority, " are more ready to talk about soul and spirit than to define theories " (**53**), so that we must not look for exact method in the beliefs recorded among the folk of the lower culture as to the nature of the soul, its relation to the body, to the phenomena of death, sleep, and the like ? Of the Andamanese we read that " they regard their reflections (in any mirror) as their souls. The colour of the soul is said to be red, and that of the spirit black and, though invisible to the human eyes, they partake of the form of the person to whom they belong. Evil emanates from the soul, and all good from the spirit : at the resurrection they will be reunited and live permanently on the new earth for the souls of the wicked will then have been reformed by the punishments inflicted on them during their residence in *jer-eg-lar-mu-gu* " (**54**). This belief in a duality of personal principle is found among the Lusheis, who hold that " each person is said to have two '*thlarao*' or souls, one of which is wise, while the other is foolish, and it is the struggle between these two that make men so unreliable " (**55**). So too the Bhutias " believe in the presence of the spirits of the dead. They are of two kinds. One is visible and anthropomorphic with a black skin ; the other is invisible, but so fatal that if its shadow falls in a man he is sure to die " (**56**). The Oraons hold that " every man has two shades. As the shadow of man projected on the wall is double, one very thick in front and the other very light a little behind, so a dead man has two shades, the heavy one that goes to *Markha*, or the heaven of the Oraons, and the other one that remains among them " (**57**). The Birhor " has two souls—a male and a female. These remain united in death as in life, and when they finally lose their present body by death, are reincarnated together in a new body. . . . The souls of a deceased Birhor need not always be reborn in his own tribe. Thus, on the very day that the Naya of a certain Birhor settlement died, a son was born to a man of the Kurmi caste in the neighbouring village. And the son of the deceased Birhor and all his tanda people seriously assured me that the Kurmi's son is the reincarnation of their old Naya " (**58**). On the other hand, the Kols believe that " Da das eigentliche Ich, das geistseelische Leben des Menschen mit dem Tode nicht vernichtet wird, sondern fort existiert und auch eine Hülle, eine Art schattenhaften Körper behält, so muss auch für seinen Lebensunterhalt im dunklen Jenseits, selbst fur Beschäftigung, ja sogar für Erholung gesorgt werden " (**59**). By reason of the intimacy of the relation of the soul or souls with the body, Santals are branded with the *sika*, so that they may be recognised on death; women are tattooed among the Tangkhuls, Abors, Daflas and the Gonds (**60**), because "the marks are the only thing that does" go to heaven. The short, dark-skinned Thanda Pulayans, whose womenfolk still wear the leaf aprons from which the tribe gets its name, say that the spirits of deceased ancestors manifest themselves in dreams, especially to near relations who speak in the morning of what they have seen in the night. They build a "little temple about the size of a large rabbit hutch in which, as a plank for the spirits of the deceased ancestors to come and rest upon. The spirits are supposed to fish in the backwaters and the phosphorescence, sometimes seen on the surface of the water, is taken as an indication of their presence" (**61**). The Gonds, too, know that "ghosts cannot squat on the bare ground like human beings, and must be given something to sit on (**62**). The ghosts of Tangkhul Nagas come and sit on stone slabs during their occasional visits to view the rice fields (**63**). Dr. Busby would have been at home among ghosts of this description.

What is it, soul or what, which in Lushai belief, so we are told (**64**), is "reincarnated in the form of hornets, and sometimes in the form of dew, and if this falls on a person the spirit is re-born in his or her child?" A similar belief is recorded as held by the Angamis, who seem to have now outgrown the idea (**65**). Among the Semas we find strange effects produced by the belief in a separable soul. There are men whose souls at times prefer some temporary shelter to the real home, so that the owner falls ill because this unstable element in his composition has deserted his body and must be called back to resume its duty, exactly what happens at times to a Lushai when one of his souls gets lost (**66**). Here, too, are men and women whose souls enter the living bodies of leopards or tiger cats, or it may be of tigers, whereof proof is certain. Tie up the man and the beast will die. Kill the beast and the man will die. "The son of Yemithi of Lizotomi, whose leopard-cat body was killed at Sagami, heard the news as he was returning to his village, and expired on the spot for no other reason. A curious example of the power of the Sema mind over the Sema body" (**67**). The Sema soul after death "may sometimes take the form of a particular hawk, probably a Kestrel . . . and the soul of the dead is not permanently embodied in the kestrel form. This much is clear, though otherwise the eschatology of the Semas is a little mixed" (**69**).

Here and there are tales which explains how death came to the world, whose meaning has been explained by Sir James Frazer (**69a**). Thus the Kabui Nagas say there was once a time when men did not die, for there was a wonderful tree whose bark would cure all ills, would even bring the dead back to life. One day the children brought the bark from the wrapping in which it was kept inside, and put it in the sun while they played. The sun stole it, knowing full well its wondrous power. Their faithful dog rushed after the thief and ate him up. But so powerful was the medicine of the bark that the sun recovered even after this rough treatment. Since then men have died because they no longer know the tree of life. Yet the sun from time to time is chased by the hound and eaten, and is always able to return to life. Thus the Kabuis explain eclipses and the death of man. For the Birhor death came into the world by a dirty trick. Men's souls would leave them and wander forth as they do now, but always returned to their body. One day a soul was returning and met a centipede, who bade him count his legs. Every time the soul tried to get his count right the centipede moved on and so the count was never finished and the soul did not return. So now men die (**70**).

The story runs that death came to the Kachins as a result of the man's disobedience towards the Lady Sun, a beneficent spirit who holds the strings of life. Angered by their deceit she ordered that old, white-haired men should suffer this penalty, but her words were marred in transmission by an evil spirit, so that death now visits young and old alike (71). So there are ways and means of ascertaining how, why and whence death has come. Men, too, have learnt subtle ways of bringing death to those they hate. Among the Khasis, three days of tabu are kept by the whole family and three eggs broken to ascertain what was the cause of death. After the funeral " Early next morning the relatives and friends go to the cairn with fresh food and water and look about for new footprints, the idea being that from these footprints they can foretell future events. This they do until the third night after the ceremony. During these three nights the front door of the house formerly occupied by the deceased is never closed, it being thought that the spirit may wish to return and visit its earthly abode (72).

Among the Kols a similar rite gives knowledge of the fate of the soul. " Nach Entfernung der Leiche wird da, wo sie lag, Asche gestreut und dann die Haustür fest verschlossen. Ist die Oberfläche der Asche nach der Rückkehr unverandert, dann ist die abgeschiedene Seele sicherlich nicht mehr in Hause. Es können aber Fälle vorkommen, in denen ein Huhn oder eine Katze über die Asche läuft, und dann ist die Sache schlimm, besonders wenn Spuren von Katzenpfoten auf der Asche zu sehen sind. In diesem Falle ist nämlich der Verstorbene ohne Zweifel zu einem bösen Geist geworden " (73).

Among the Gonds, " In Bastar, on some selected day, a short time after the death, they obtain two small baskets and set them out at night, placing a chicken under the one, and some flour of wheat under the other. The householder then says, " I do the work of those old men who died. O spirits, I offer a chicken to you : be true and I will perform your funeral rites to-morrow." On the next morning the basket placed over the flour is lifted up, and if a mark resembling a footprint of a man or any animal be found, they think that the deceased has become incarnate in a human being or that animal" (**74**).

The Birhors spread ashes over the spot where the dead man breathed his last, and if there are footprints found on them know that footprints like those of a person entering the hut mean that death was caused by a spirit of the house, while "if footprints like those of a person going out of the hut, it is concluded that it is some outside spirit, perhaps one of a different tanda, which is responsible for the death" (**75**). Thus indications of the future, proofs of the state and whereabouts of the soul, evidence of the cause of death, can be ascertained. The ghost or spirit helps in these delicate matters, and even more directly forces upon his late fellows the knowledge which they seek.

And among the Gonds (**76**) "the bearers with the body on their shoulders face round to the west and about **10** yards in front of them are placed three saj leaves in a line with a space of a yard between each, the first representing the supreme being, the second disembodied spirits and the third witchcraft. Sometimes a little rice is put on the leaves. An axe is struck three times on the ground, and a villager now cries to the deceased to disclose the cause of his death, and immediately the bearers, impelled as they believe by the dead man, carry the body to one of the leaves. If they halt before the first, then the death was in the course of nature; if before the second, it arose from the anger of offended spirits; if before the third witchcraft was the cause. The ordeal may be thrice repeated, the arrangement of the leaves being changed each time. If witchcraft is indicated as the cause of death and confirmed by the repeated tests, the corpse is asked to point out the sorcerer or witch, and the body is carried along until it halts before some one in the crowd who is at once seized and disposed of as a witch. Sometimes the corpse may be carried to the house of a witch in another village to a distance of 8 or 10 miles. In Mandla in such cases a Gunia or exorciser formerly called on the corpse to go forward and point out the witch. The bearers then, impelled by the corpse, made one step forward and stopped. The exorciser then again adjured the corpse, and the bearers made a step and this was repeated again and again until they halted in front of the supposed witch. All the beholders and the bearers themselves thus thought they were impelled by the corpse and the episode is a good illustration of the power of suggestion. Frequently the detected witch was one of the deceased's wives. In Mandla the cause of the man's death was determined by the digging of his grave. When piling in the earth removed for the grave after burial, if it reached exactly to the surface of the ground, they thought that the dead man had died after living the proper span of his life. If the earth made a mound over the hole, they thought he had lived beyond his allotted time and called him *Sigpur*, that is a term for a measure of grain heaped as high as it will stand over the brim. But if the earth was insufficient and did not reach to the level of the ground, they held that he had been prematurely cut off and had been killed by an enemy or by a witch through magic."

Let us then follow the soul in its destination as beliefs in the lower culture depict that place for us. For the Andamanese " the whole area under the earth is a gloomy place, *Cha-it-an* whither the spirits of the departed are sent by Puluga to await the resurrection." No change takes place in *cha-it-an* in respect to growth or age; all remain as they were at the time of their departure from the earth, and the adults are represented as engaged in hunting after a manner peculiar to disembodied spirits. . . , Between the earth and the eastern sky there stretches an invisible cane bridge which steadies the former and connects it with *jer-eg* or paradise ; over this bridge the souls (*ot-yo-lo*) of the departed pass into paradise or to *jer-eglar-mu-gu,* which is situated below it; this latter place might be described as Purgatory for it is a place of punishment for those who have been guilty of heinous sins such as murder. Like Dante they depict it as very cold and therefore a most undesirable region for mortals to inhabit. . . . The future life will be but a repetition of the present, but all will then remain in the prime of life, and sickness and death will be unknown; and there will be no more marrying or giving in marriage (**77**).

For the Garo there is a "kind of purgatory through which all must pass, the good and the bad alike. As the mortal worked on earth, so the spirit must work at *Chikmang.* On arrival there he inquires the whereabouts of the relations who have gone before him, builds his house where they built, or lives with them if they have not yet returned to earthly life. Spirit-land is not in any sense a place of joy and a speedy release with a happy reincarnation is hoped for" (**78**).

The Lushais "believe in a spirit world beyond the grave which is known as *Mithikua—i.e.,* dead man's village—but on the far side of Mi-thi-kua runs the Pial River, beyond which lies Pielral; an abode of bliss. Access to this is not obtained by a life of virtue while on earth, but by the due performance of sacrifices and the killing of men and certain animals and success in the courts of Venus. . . ." (**79**).

Garo, Lushai and Naga believe that the path to the abode of the spirits is guarded by a demon who may be tricked, who may be overcome in fair fight, who is bound to let pass the fortunate whose duty had been duly done as warrior, hunter, giver of feasts or as lover. "Women whoever they may be, he always shoots at" (**80**). For the Lushai religion is essentially man-made. The wily Garo ministers to the greed of the demon and hurls a pile of brass ear-rings at its feet and gets to safety (**81**). The Mao Naga is armed with spears to meet this enemy

(82), while the Sema adds to his spear a peg-top and secures a passage for his women-folk who "delude *Lolave* when she comes to the narrow where he lies in wait for passing souls seeking whom he may devour. He sits in the path with a truculent air. 'My head is full of lice,' says he. 'Oh,' says she, 'let me kill them for you.' Then she goes up and as he sits there searches his head and starts to click the bamboo slip from time to time as though it were the popping of squashed lice, monsters in size. Suddenly she flicks the bean to a distance. 'I will go and catch it,' she says, and so slips by and escapes. In the same way a man or boy gets by when pretending to go to fetch his errant peg-top" **(83)**. For the Santal, as for the Garo, heaven offers but a repetition of toil and trouble, since "All the spirits are employed in grinding the bones of past generations with a pestle made of the wood of the castor oil tree in order to provide the gods with a good supply of material to produce the children yet unborn" **(84)**.

Thus death may come "in the course of nature" by the action of powerful disembodied spirits, by the power of evil man. It may come automatically as the result of the infraction of a social tabu, for with the Semas a breach of the etiquette between maternal uncle and nephew "is believed to entail its own penalty of serious misfortune or death" **(85)**. "Sickness, sin and death," as I wrote some time ago, "are not for them isolated unconnected phenomena. Sin, in their view, consists primarily of breaches, both by accident and intent, of the unwritten law of society. What gives validity to these unwritten laws is the vague fear that something may happen if they are broken" **(86)**.

Nor in the face of some such breach is the community forced to sit down and meekly await the day of destiny, for it may, in self-protection, act so as to secure that the guilty person suffers in his own person. Among the Angamis "The observation of penna or kenna by the village may cause the death of a person named as its subject. . . . In the other case mentioned, that of the Nerhema man who sacrificed a black cat, the village actually observed a day's penna with the hope and intention of making his illness worse. There is, however, a procedure more effective than the mere holding of a penna alone. On the day of penna a sort of Commination Service may be held to curse some unfortunate who has given offence. The Kemovo gets up before the assembled clan, all the children being present, and announces that So-and-so has done such and such a deed, whereon the people answer, 'Sa, sa,' 'Let him die, let him die.' This curse is believed to be a powerful one and to strengthen it still further a branch of green leaves is put up to represent the person cursed, and everyone hurls spears of wood or bamboo at the bough with expressions as 'Let him die,' 'Kill So-and-so,' and every sort of abuse. The spears are left where they lie, the bough withers and the subject of the curse dies likewise. This performance is also held to be effective even when the name of the culprit is unknown" (**87**).

The theory of the causation of death where the course of nature is excluded, rests in part at least on the vulnerability of the soul to attacks by spirits or by evil men. In like manner sickness is explained now as due to the temporary desertion of the body by the soul (here viewed as the principle of life and normal conditions), again as due to the activity of spirits of sickness, shading into a material theory of causation, since folk like "The Angamis conceive of the spirit of smallpox as sowing the disease, as it were seeds, over all entering in at the village gate" (**88**). And it is caused by malevolent maleficent human agencies. Treatment and theory are not to be separated. Diagnosis with so difficult a theory to handle is a matter for the expert, and it is for this reason that we have the strange combination of witch-finder and healer, diviner and doctor, as in the Naga Themuma, whose "powers vary from merely dreaming dreams to the practice of genuine black magic " (89), since he who can cure disease can also cause disease, or, as in the Oraon Ojha, whose " office " consists in finding out the *bhuts* that cause sickness and in tracing the witches at whose behest the evil spirits have set to work. Just as there are dreams whose meaning and interpretation are matters of common form, so there are sicknesses which all know how to treat, certain ailments with specific remedies, some of real use and others literally ordered on the principle of using a " hair of the dog that bit you " (90). Nor are prophylactic measures unknown to the lower culture, since " Disease may also be averted by offering a substitute in the form of old cloths, live chickens, eggs, etc. . . . . Chickens freed and driven away in the jungle to serve as a substitute for the person turning them away (or perhaps merely as an offering for the spirits of the jungle or, it may be, to carry away the element of sickness or misfortune that attaches to the persons who devote them to this purpose) are called *chesu* and regarded as accursed " (91). I have seen a maiba extract, or claim to extract, by sleight of hand, a fragment of stone from a Naga suffering from fever and the patient is markedly relieved by the operation. " Sufficeth it that the thumomi believes in himself, and is believed in by his patients, and in very truth often cures them by faith alone " (92).

As there are Gods whose business it is to give the rain, so are there rites to be performed by man to secure the rain if it be withheld and in a land where man depends on a regular, equably distributed rainfall at the due season, many are the devices by which the powers that be are reminded of or constrained to their duty. Sacrifices are offered, solemn communal rites have to be celebrated, as among the Semas, who charge the village sexton with the task, which consists in getting a huluks head, filling it with pounded seed in place of the brains, and then sticks it in a deep pool on a stake. " When enough rain has fallen they remove the head and pull out the stake, otherwise the rain would fall continuously " (**93**). Again " Others drown a pig in the nearest pool, having first tied its feet together. I once noticed some bits of fish lying about on the village dam, and asked why they were put there. I learnt that there had been a water or rain ceremony. . . . In one village I was told that when rain was wanted the headman takes a burning brand from the fire and places it on the grave of a man who has died of burns and then quenches it with water and calls for rain " (**94**), a clear case of utilising the ghost of the man for social purposes. The women, too, have their rites whereby they may help in need.

Nor are things without powers akin to those of animate beings for there are stones " male and female that breed produce offspring yearly " (**95**).

In his exhaustive survey of totemism in India, Sir James Frazer found that " this remarkable institution, combined as usual with exogamy, is widespread among the swarthy, almost black race called Dravidian, with their squat figures, dark eyes, and broad negro-like noses, who represent the most primitive type of man in India, and occupy the oldest geological formation in the country, to wit, the medley of forest-clad ranges, terraced plateaux, and undulating plains which stretches from the Vindhya mountains on the north to Cape Comorin on the south. Indeed the evidence seems to justify us in inferring that at one time or another totemism and exogamy have been practised by all the branches of this numerous and ancient people. . . . . It appears doubtful whether totemism proper is practised by any race of India except the Dravidian. We have indeed found some resemblances to it in combination with exogamy among the Mongoloid peoples of Assam, but it is not certain that these resemblances are proof of the actual existence of the institution " (**96**). But this remarkable institution, widespread through the world, is the outcome of an attitude which "regards the animals or plants or whatever the totem may be, as his friends or relations, his fathers, his brothers, and so forth. He puts them as far as he can on a footing of equality with himself and with his fellows, the members of the same totemic clan" (**97**). In the belief in the weretiger, whose dewlaps prove his humanity, in the lycanthropist who dies when his tiger self is killed, in the group tabus which in the lower culture bind the human groups so intimately that what happens to one affects all that belong, or may in time belong, to that group, I find evidence of the attitude of mind which goes with and underlies totemism, in those areas in India where totemism is not.

All over India many cases of group tabus can be found among peoples who are not commonly deemed totemic. Thus the Banyok of Upper Burma do not use gold or silver or precious stones, while on the other side of India, in Baluchistan, certain Umrani Baloch deliberately refrain from plastering their roofs because they say one of their forefathers died under a plastered roof. The sanction of these tabus is the belief that if violated death, sickness or some calamity will happen either to the violator, or to some one of his group. Wherever group consciousness is strong, and belief in the power of "things to affect human beings is flourishing, these group tabus readily originate and persists" (**98**). The border line between the natural and supernatural, between man and the rest of the world, is hard to trace. Frail is the constitution of man, delicately poised and balanced ; fearfully and wonderfully made is he, truly the sport of circumstance, in body and in mind, so that whatever is strange is apt to be viewed by him as dangerous. The partnership of body and soul is fatal to both, for they are so intertwined in life that violence to the one will hurt and may even destroy the other. A little knowledge is indeed a dangerous thing. So we come back to the point we marked as our start that the lower culture is what it is by reason of its psychology, of its strong faith in the value of dreams and abnormal impressions, its traditionalist attitude and therefore its timidity towards the new and unfamiliar. Its mode of thought is concrete, but it enlarges the domain of the concrete, for it sees reality and revelation where we see but the baseless fabric of a dream. They are human as we are, know pain and grief as we know them, and their minds are active even as ours on the problems which are problems still for us. They fashion their replies in their own manner.

The lower culture lives, is active, is the perennial source whence new inspiration, new vigour, are derived ; it is the basis of human societies, for it holds together in virtue of the strength of the social consciousness, and its group unity.

1. *Tribes and Castes of the Central Provinces*, vol. i., p. 109.
2. *The Garos*, p. 100.
3. *The Naga Tribes of Manipur*, p. 143.
4. Colonel McCulloch, *Account of Munnipore*, p. 51.
5. *The Khasis*, p. 125.
6. *Gebiet der Kols Mission*, p. 72.
7. *Memoirs of the Asiatic Society of Bengal*, vol. i., No. 9, p. 154.
8. Census Report, 1911, vol. v., p. 331.
9. *Journal of the Bihar and Orissa Research Society*, December ,1919, p. 621.
10. *The Sema Nagas*, p. 237.
11. *The Story of an Indian Upland*, p. 285.
12. *Descriptive Ethnology of Bengal*, p. 39 ; *Things Indian*, p. 462.
13. *Ethnographic Notes in Southern India*, p. 366 *sq*.
14. *Castes and Tribes of S. India*, vol. ii., p. 39, vol. vii., p. 423.
15. *Tribes and Castes of the Central Provinces*, vol. iii., p. 72.
16. Census Report, 1901, vol. iii., p. 65.
17. *The Andaman Islanders*, p. 77.
18. *Gebiet der Kols Mission*, p. 81.
19. *Tribes and Castes of Bengal*, vol. i., pp. 531, 532.
20. *The Mystic Rose*, p. 341.
21. *Encyclopaedia of Religion and Ethics*, vol. viii., p. 431.
22. *Annals of Rural Bengal*, p. 210.
23. *Story of an Indian Upland*, p. 86.
24. Ethnographic Survey of Mysore, *Bulletin* 1, p. 10.
25. *The Angami Nagas*, pp. 26, 365. *Sema Nagas*, pp. 14, 227.
26. Census Report, 1911, vol. iii., p. 141.
27. *The Naga Tribes of Manipur*, p. 188.

28. *The Todas*, p. 366.
29. *The Sema Nagas*, p. 242.
30. *Journal of the Bihar and Orissa Research Society*, December, 1919, p. 620.
31. Brown, *Account of Munnipore*, p. 115.
32. *The Angami Nagas*, p. 217.
33. Census Report, 1911, vol. v., p. 330.
34. *Ibid.*, .
35. *Castes and Tribes of Southern India*, vol. iii., p. 500.
36. *Descriptive Ethnology of Bengal*, p. 283.
37. *The Lushei Kuki Clans*, pp. 158, 164.
38. *The Angami Nagas*, p. 229.
39. Brown, *Account of Munnipore*, p. 116.
40. *Gebiet der Kols Mission*, p. 87.
41. *Memoirs of the Asiatic Society of Bengal*, vol. i., No. 9, p. 140.
42. *Tribes and Castes of the Central Provinces*, vol. i., p. 106.
43. *Linguistic Survey of India*, vol. iii., part 1, p. 5.
44. *The Angamis*, p. 177 *sq.*
45. *The Belief in Immortality*, vol. 1., p. 9.
46. *Ibid.*
47. *Ibid.*, p. 23.
48. *The Andaman Islanders*, p. 44 ; *Folklore*, xx., part 3, p. 257 *sqq.*
49. *The Sema Nagas*, p. 194.
50. *The Angamis*, p. 187 ; *The Lushei Clans*, p. 80; J.A.S.B., *Memoirs* vol. i., No. 9, p. 124.
51. *The Sema Nagas*, p. 231.
52. *Memoirs of the Asiatic Society of Bengal*, vol. i., No. 9, p. 144.
53. *Hinduism and Buddhism*, vol. i., p. lxiv.
54. *The Andaman Islanders*, p. 94.
55. *The Lushei Kuki Clans*, p. 61.
56. Census Report, 1901, vol. vi., p. 404.
57. *Memoirs of the Asiatic Society of Bengal*, vol. i., No. 9, p. 135.
58. *Journal of the Bihar and Orissa Research Society*, September, 1918, p. 309.
59. *Gebiet der Kols Mission*, p. 83.
60. *Aboriginal Tribes of the Central Provinces* (Rev. S. Hislop), p. 11.
61. *Castes and Tribes of S. India*, vol. vii., p. 27.
62. *Tribes and Castes of the Central Provinces*, vol. iii., p. 93.
63. *The Naga Tribes of Manipur*, p. 191.
64. *The Lushei Kuki Clans*, p. 65.
65. Brown's *Account of Munnipore*, p. 116 ; *The Angamis*, p. 184.
66. *The Semas*, p. 200.
67. *The Semas*, p. 199 to 206.
68. Census Report, 1911, vol. iii., p. 77.
69. *The Semas*, p. 208, 209.
69a. *The Belief in Immortality*, p. 59 *sq.*
70. *Journal of the Bihar and Orissa Research Society*, September, 1918, p. 307.
71. *Handbook of Kachin Language*, p. 143.
72. *The Khasis*, p. 135.
73. *Gebiet der Kols Mission*, p. 85.
74. *Tribes and Castes of the Central Provinces*, vol. iii., p. 94.
75. *Journal of the Bihar and Orissa Research Society*, September, 1918, p. 317
76. *Tribes and Castes of the Central Provinces*, vol. iii., p. 90.

77. *The Andaman Islanders*, pp. 93, 94.
78. *The Garos*, p. 102 *sq.*
79. *The Lushei Kuki Clans*, pp. 61 *sq.*
80. *Ibid.*, p. 62.
81. *The Garos*, pp. 103, 104.
82. *The Naga Tribes of Manipur*, p. 161.
83. *The Semas*, p. 244.
84. *Story of an Indian Upland*, p. 286.
85. *The Semas*, p. 137.
86. *Archiv für Religions wissenschaft* xii. p. 451.
87. *The Angamis*, p. 241.
88. *Ibid.*, p. 178.
89. *The Angamis*, p. 242.
90. *The Angamis*, p. 100.
91. *The Angamis*, p. 179.
92. *The Semas*, p. 232.
93. *Ibid.*, p. 215.
94. *The Naga Tribes of Manipur*, p. 169 *sq.*
95. *The Angamis*, p. 180.
96. *Totemism and Exogamy*, vol. ii., pp. 329 *sq.*
97. *Ibid.*, vol. iv., p. 4.
98. *Oxford Survey of the British Empire*, vol. ii., p. 224.

INDEX

H.

I.

J.

K.

L.

M.

N.

O.

P.

R.

S.

T.

V.

W.